ALLDATA 2019

The Fifth International Conference on Big Data, Small Data, Linked Data and Open Data

March 24 - 28, 2019

Valencia, Spain

ALLDATA 2019 Editors

Claus-Peter Rückemann, Westfälische Wilhelms-Universität Münster (WWU) and DIMF and Leibniz Universität Hannover, Germany

Printed from e-media with permission by:

Curran Associates, Inc.
57 Morehouse Lane
Red Hook, NY 12571

Some format issues inherent in the e-media version may also appear in this print version.

Printed by Curran Associates, Inc. (2019)

International Academy, Research, and Industry Association (IARIA)
412 Derby Way
Wilmington, DE 19810

Phone: (408) 893-6407
Fax: (408) 527-6351

petre@iaria.org

Additional copies of this publication are available from:

Curran Associates, Inc.
57 Morehouse Lane
Red Hook, NY 12571 USA
Phone: 845-758-0400
Fax: 845-758-2633
Email: curran@proceedings.com
Web: www.proceedings.com

Table of Contents

ALLDATA 2019

Forward

The Fifth International Conference on Big Data, Small Data, Linked Data and Open Data (ALLDATA 2019), held between March 24, 2019 and March 28, 2019 in Valencia, Spain, continued a series of events bridging the concepts and the communities devoted to each of data categories for a better understanding of data semantics and their use, by taking advantage from the development of Semantic Web, Deep Web, Internet, non-SQL and SQL structures, progresses in data processing, and the new tendency for acceptance of open environments.

The volume and the complexity of available information overwhelm human and computing resources. Several approaches, technologies and tools are dealing with different types of data when searching, mining, learning and managing existing and increasingly growing information. From understanding Small data, the academia and industry recently embraced Big data, Linked data, and Open data. Each of these concepts carries specific foundations, algorithms and techniques, and is suitable and successful for different kinds of application. While approaching each concept from a silo point of view allows a better understanding (and potential optimization), no application or service can be developed without considering all data types mentioned above.

We welcomed academic, research and industry contributions. The conference had the following tracks:

- Big Data
- Open Data
- Linked Data
- Challenges in processing Big Data and applications

We take here the opportunity to warmly thank all the members of the ALLDATA 2019 technical program committee, as well as all the reviewers. The creation of such a high quality conference program would not have been possible without their involvement. We also kindly thank all the authors who dedicated much of their time and effort to contribute to ALLDATA 2019. We truly believe that, thanks to all these efforts, the final conference program consisted of top quality contributions.

We also thank the members of the ALLDATA 2019 organizing committee for their help in handling the logistics and for their work that made this professional meeting a success.

We hope that ALLDATA 2019 was a successful international forum for the exchange of ideas and results between academia and industry and to promote further progress in the field of all data. We also hope that Valencia, Spain provided a pleasant environment during the conference and everyone saved some time to enjoy the historic charm of the city.

ALLDATA 2019 Chairs

ALLDATA Steering Committee

Venkat N. Gudivada, East Carolina University, USA

Sandjai Bhulai, Vrije Universiteit Amsterdam, the Netherlands
Jerzy Grzymala-Busse, University of Kansas, USA
Fabrice Mourlin, Université Paris-Est Créteil Val de Marne, France
Andrzej Skowron, Warsaw University, Poland

ALLDATA Industry/Research Advisory Committee
Stephane Puechmorel, ENAC, France
Cyril Onwubiko, Research Series Ltd., London, UK
Hanmin Jung [정한민], Korea Institute of Science and Technology Information, South Korea

ALLDATA 2019 Special Tracks Chair
Miran Taha, University of Sulaimani, Kurdistan Region, Irak

ALLDATA 2019
Committee

ALLDATA Steering Committee

Venkat N. Gudivada, East Carolina University, USA
Sandjai Bhulai, Vrije Universiteit Amsterdam, the Netherlands
Jerzy Grzymala-Busse, University of Kansas, USA
Fabrice Mourlin, Université Paris-Est Créteil Val de Marne, France
Andrzej Skowron, Warsaw University, Poland

ALLDATA Industry/Research Advisory Committee

Stephane Puechmorel, ENAC, France
Cyril Onwubiko, Research Series Ltd., London, UK
Hanmin Jung [정한민], Korea Institute of Science and Technology Information, South Korea

ALLDATA 2019 Special Tracks Chair

Miran Taha, University of Sulaimani, Kurdistan Region, Irak

ALLDATA 2019 Technical Program Committee

Maurizio Atzori, University of Cagliari, Italy
Akhilesh Bajaj, University of Tulsa, USA
Houda Bakir, CEREP - Ecole National Supérieur d'ingénieurs de Tunis / Datavora, Tunisia
Ken Barker, University of Calgary, Canada
Gábor Bella, University of Trento, Italy / University of Edinburgh, UK
Valerio Bellandi, Università degli Studi di Milano, Italy
Sandjai Bhulai, Vrije Universiteit Amsterdam, Netherlands
Keith Chan, The Hong Kong Polytechnic University, Hong Kong
Rachid Chelouah, EISTI, France
Yue Chen, Palo Alto Networks, USA
Roger H. L. Chiang, University of Cincinnati, USA
Esma Nur Cinicioglu, Istanbul University, Turkey
Carmela Comito, National Research Council of Italy (CNR) - Institute for High Performance Computing and Networking, Italy
Cinzia Daraio, Sapienza University of Rome, Italy
Maaike de Boer, TNO, Netherlands
Maria Cristina De Cola, IRCCS Centro Neurolesi "Bonino-Pulejo", Messina, Italy
Konstantinos Demertzis, Eastern Macedonia & Thrace Institute of Technology, Greece
Christian Dirschl, Wolters Kluwer Deutschland GmbH, Germany
Süleyman Eken, Kocaeli University, Turkey
Mounîm A. El Yacoubi, Telecom SudParis, France
Rania El-Gazzar, Universty of South-Eastern Norway, Norway
Nadia Essoussi, University of Carthage, Tunisia

Jolon Faichney, Griffith University, Australia
Denise Beatriz Ferrari, Instituto Tecnológico de Aeronáutica, São José dos Campos - SP, Brazil
Paola Festa, University of Napoli FEDERICO II, Italy
Sandro Fonseca de Souza, Universidade do Estado do Rio de Janeiro, Brazil / CERN - European Laboratory for Particle Physics, Swizerland
Fausto Pedro Garcia Márquez, University of Castilla-La Mancha, Spain
Ilias Gialampoukidis, Information Technologies Institute | Centre of Research & Technology - Hellas (ITI-CERTH), Greece
Ana González-Marcos, Universidad de La Rioja, Spain
Jerzy Grzymala-Busse, University of Kansas, USA
Venkat N. Gudivada, East Carolina University, USA
Didem Gürdür, KTH Royal Institute of Technology, Stockholm, Sweden
Tzung-Pei Hong, National University of Kaohsiung, Taiwan
Wen-Chi Hou, Southern Illinois University, USA
Tsan-sheng Hsu, Academia Sinica, Taiwan
Jaroslaw Jankowski, West Pomeranian University of Technology, Poland
Hanmin Jung, Korea Institute of Science and Technology Information, South Korea
David Kaeli, Northeastern University, USA
Eleni Kaldoudi, Democritus University of Thrace, Greece
Sokratis K. Katsikas, Norwegian University of Science & Technology (NTNU), Norway
Rasib Khan, Northern Kentucky University, USA
Dimitris Kontokostas, University of Leipzig, Germany
Alexander P. Kuleshov, Skolkovo Institute of Science and Technology (Skoltech), Russia
Alexander Lazovik, University of Groningen, Netherlands
Jerry Chun-Wei Lin, Harbin Institute of Technology Shenzhen Graduate School, Chinas
Iryna Lishchuk, Institut für Rechtsinformatik - Leibniz Universität Hannover
Angelica Lo Duca, Institute of Informatics and Telematics, National Research Council (IIT-CNR), Italy
Xiaoyi Lu, Ohio State University, USA
Wencan Luo, University of Pittsburgh, USA
Yutao Ma, Wuhan University, China
Imen Megdiche, Université Paul Sabatier, France
Armando B. Mendes, Universidade dos Açores, Portugal
Shegaw Mengiste, Universty of South-Eastern Norway, Norway
Óscar Mortágua Pereira, University of Aveiro, Portugal
Fabrice Mourlin, Université Paris-Est Créteil Val de Marne, France
Emir Muñoz, Fujitsu Ltd. / Insight Centre for Data Analytics at NUI Galway, Ireland
Fionn Murtagh, University of Huddersfield, UK
Georges Mykoniatis, ENAC LAB, France
Saurabh Nagrecha, Center for Machine Learning at Capital One, USA
Hidemoto Nakada, National Institute of Advanced Industrial Science and Technology (AIST), Japan
Sangha Nam, KAIST, Korea
Florence Nicol, Ecole Nationale de l'Aviation Civile, France

Sadegh Nobari, Rakuten Inc., Japan
Cyril Onwubiko, Research Series Ltd., London, UK
Ren-Hao Pan, Yuan Ze University, Taiwan
Jisha Jose Panackal, Sacred Heart College, Kerala, India
Luca Pappalardo, University of Pisa, Germany
Francesco Pascale, University of Salerno, Italy
Antonio Picariello, University of Naples Federico II, Italy
Spyros E. Polykalas, Technological Educational Institute of Ionian Islands, Greece
Livia Predoiu, University of Oxford, UK
Stephane Puechmorel, ENAC, France
Zbigniew W. Ras, University of North Carolina, USA
Yehezkel Resheff, Hebrew University, Jerusalem, Israel
Ivan Rodero, Rutgers University, USA
Paolo Romano, University of Lisbon / INESC-ID, Portugal
Giulio Rossetti, Istituto di Scienza e Tecnologie dell'Informazione "A. Faedo" - National Research Council, Italy
Peter Ruppel, Technische Universität Berlin, Germany
Jedrzej Rybicki, Supercomputing Center Juelich, Germany
David Sánchez, Universitat Rovira i Virgili, Spain
Stefanie Scherzinger, OTH Regensburg, Germany
Monica M. L. Sebillo, University of Salerno, Italy
Suzanne Michelle Shontz, University of Kansas, USA
Andrzej Skowron, Warsaw University, Poland
Marek Śmieja, Jagiellonian University, Poland
Srivathsan Srinivasagopalan, Visa Inc., USA
Bela Stantic, Griffith University, Australia
Uta Störl, University of Applied Sciences Darmstadt, Germany
Hung-Min Sun, National Tsing Hua University, Taiwan
Zbigniew Suraj, University of Rzeszów, Poland
George Tambouratzis, Institute for Language and Speech Processing, Greece
Vahid Taslimitehrani, PhysioSigns Inc., USA
Maurizio Tesconi, Institute of Informatics and Telematics - CNR, Italy
Hadi Fanaee Tork, University of Oslo, Norway
Ismail Hakki Toroslu, Middle East Technical University, Turkey
Christos Tryfonopoulos, University of the Peloponnese, Greece
Chrisa Tsinaraki, European Commission - Joint Research Centre, Italy
Michael Vassilakopoulos, University of Thessaly, Greece
Thanasis Vergoulis, Information Management Systems Institute - "Athena" Research Center, Greece
Hironori Washizaki, Waseda University, Japan
Ouri Wolfson, University of Illinois, USA
Lei Xu, Shanghai Jiao Tong University, China
Feng George Yu, Youngstown State University, USA
Fouad Zablith, American University of Beirut, Lebanon

Bo Zhang, IBM, USA
Li Zhang, Northumbria University, Newcastle, UK
Qiang Zhu, University of Michigan, USA

Copyright Information

For your reference, this is the text governing the copyright release for material published by IARIA.

The copyright release is a transfer of publication rights, which allows IARIA and its partners to drive the dissemination of the published material. This allows IARIA to give articles increased visibility via distribution, inclusion in libraries, and arrangements for submission to indexes.

I, the undersigned, declare that the article is original, and that I represent the authors of this article in the copyright release matters. If this work has been done as work-for-hire, I have obtained all necessary clearances to execute a copyright release. I hereby irrevocably transfer exclusive copyright for this material to IARIA. I give IARIA permission or reproduce the work in any media format such as, but not limited to, print, digital, or electronic. I give IARIA permission to distribute the materials without restriction to any institutions or individuals. I give IARIA permission to submit the work for inclusion in article repositories as IARIA sees fit.

I, the undersigned, declare that to the best of my knowledge, the article is does not contain libelous or otherwise unlawful contents or invading the right of privacy or infringing on a proprietary right.

Following the copyright release, any circulated version of the article must bear the copyright notice and any header and footer information that IARIA applies to the published article.

IARIA grants royalty-free permission to the authors to disseminate the work, under the above provisions, for any academic, commercial, or industrial use. IARIA grants royalty-free permission to any individuals or institutions to make the article available electronically, online, or in print.

IARIA acknowledges that rights to any algorithm, process, procedure, apparatus, or articles of manufacture remain with the authors and their employers.

I, the undersigned, understand that IARIA will not be liable, in contract, tort (including, without limitation, negligence), pre-contract or other representations (other than fraudulent misrepresentations) or otherwise in connection with the publication of my work.

Exception to the above is made for work-for-hire performed while employed by the government. In that case, copyright to the material remains with the said government. The rightful owners (authors and government entity) grant unlimited and unrestricted permission to IARIA, IARIA's contractors, and IARIA's partners to further distribute the work.

Research of Topics Discovery and Tech Evolution Based on Text Preprocessed Latent Dirichlet Allocation Model

Research Topic Analysis in GaN Tech Field

Wang Li[1, 2], Shen Xiang[1,2], Liu Xiwen[1, 2]
[1]National Science Library, Chinese Academy of Sciences
[2] Department of Library, Information and Archives Management,
University of Chinese Academy of Sciences
Beijing, China
E-mail: {wangle, shenx, liuxw}@mail.las.ac.cn

***Abstract*—Computational Science and Data Science are inspiring the intelligent analysis and information service today. Machine learning text analysis is changing the traditional analysis methods. This article discusses the benefits of unsupervised learning approaches in patent text mining. Patent data of GaN industry were preprocessed by filter model based on NLTK Toolkit to identify the tech terms and then clustered them based on Latent Dirichlet Allocation model to find the latent topics which were visualized. Based on group operation, new emerging terms ranked by TFIDF through every year were used to reveal the research and development focused evolution. This research offers a demonstration of the proposed method based on 26,854 GaN patents. The results show 20 Research and Development topics with tech terms in GaN industry and present a Research and Development focus evolution based on new emerging terms every year, which provides a clue for more detaied analyses later. Our results show an efficent way to find technology focused evolution from a large scale text data.**

Keywords- LDA; automatic term identification; preprocessed text; visualization.

I. INTRODUCTION

As an unsupervised learning method, the Latent Dirichlet Allocation (LDA) is widely used for topics finding in large text analysis. Topic model is a generative model for documents which are mixtures of topics comprising words over probability distribution. Traditionally, words were used to construct an LDA model, which resulted in quite a lot of general words on top of each topic. Herein, the noun terms are utilized instead of words to discover patterns of term-use and the documents relationship.

In the Derwent Innovation Index (DII) database, original patent titles and abstracts are rewritten in English and the technology details including patent novelty, use, advantage and so on from patent full text are extracted. In this paper, based on preprocessed text dataset of 26,854 patent titles and abstracts about GaN technology field from DII, the research topics were discovered, and R&D focus changes were detected and visualized.

Researches about R&D changes or evolution based on LDA have focuses at topic level. T. L.Griffiths et al. write about a method identifying 'hot topics' or 'cold topics' [1]. D. Choi et al. explore technological trends based on patent share and their change at the topic level [2]. X. C. Gong et al. detect topic splitting and merging based on the LDA Model [3]. J. B. Qu et al. analyze topic evolution with topic relevance from adjacent time intervals [4]. Many researches have improved and practiced methods detecting R&D changes or evolution at topic level, while few have discussed finer granularity analyzing at term level.

II. TEXT PREPROCESSING

Since most terms have the syntactic form of a noun phrase [5], identifying the noun phrases in the text was executed during text preprocessing. Part-Of-Speech Tagging in Python NLTK was used to construct language filter and identify noun phrases as following:

1. The sequence consists of nouns, v-ing form and adjectives, such as the phrase 'device comprising virtual display system'.
2. The sequence ends with a noun or a v-ing form, such as the phrase 'distributing workflow' or 'business computing.

Additionally, stop contents were manipulated in the Python script from three different levels: sentence, phrase and word. For example, the publisher information sentence such as '(C) 2018 Elsevier B.V. All rights reserved' and the patent text description phrases such as 'independent claim' were stopped. Basically, uppercase and lowercase, singular and plural nouns and so on are preprocessed on word level.

After text preprocessing, the terms were prepared for LDA model.

III. RESEARCH TOPICS FINDING AND VISUALIZING

A. Research Topics Finding

The Gibbs sampling algorithm was used, with β =0.1, α =50/T, (T is the number of topics) [6]. In practical application, β is relatively small and words can be expected into a specific research topic [1]. Since GaN field is already a specific area, fewer topics are involved in this case. Because the value of T in is very small, less than 30, topics for different T were discriminated manually to avoid overlap between topics in macro level. Finally, 20 topics were suitable for GaN patent data, as shown in Table 1.

TABLE I. GAN RESEARCH TOPICS BASED ON LDA MODEL

Topic1	Score	Topic 2	Score	Topic 3	Score
layer	0.0919	substrate	0.0167	gate electrode	0.0258
gallium	0.0428	material	0.0097	drain electrode	0.0192
buffer layer	0.0399	diode	0.0077	source electrode	0.0177
substrate	0.0344	array	0.0066	source	0.0165
aluminum	0.0192	device	0.0061	barrier layer	0.0163
Topic 4	**score**	**Topic 5**	**score**	**Topic 6**	**score**
active layer	0.0632	substrate	0.0676	quantum dot	0.0066
light emitting device	0.0241	growing	0.0161	gallium arsenide	0.0057
emitting device	0.0197	layer	0.0133	indium	0.0054
semiconductor layer	0.0167	gallium	0.0111	composition	0.0051
p-type semiconductor layer	0.0150	epitaxial layer	0.0105	indium phosphide	0.0049
Topic 7	**score**	**Topic 8**	**score**	**Topic 9**	**score**
substrate	0.0185	layer	0.0188	light	0.0168
temperature	0.0162	manufacture	0.0165	wavelength	0.0104
growing	0.0115	nitride semiconductor layer	0.0148	light source	0.0074
nitrogen	0.0098	group	0.0107	light-emitting device	0.0071
heating	0.0089	thickness	0.0094	phosphor	0.0052
Topic 10	**score**	**Topic 11**	**score**	**Topic 12**	**score**
group	0.0507	forming	0.0407	aluminum	0.0277
crystal	0.0205	substrate	0.0337	silicon	0.0245
manufacture	0.0192	surface	0.0180	titanium	0.0142
gallium	0.0140	etching	0.0152	silicon carbide	0.0138
single crystal	0.0108	removing	0.0099	zinc	0.0137
Topic 13	**score**	**Topic 14**	**score**	**Topic 15**	**score**
substrate	0.0276	device	0.0216	substrate	0.0242
active layer	0.0111	diode	0.0095	second electrode	0.0104
semiconductor laser	0.0109	semiconductor element	0.0079	material	0.0102
surface	0.0105	circuit	0.0070	first electrode	0.0093
direction	0.0097	anode	0.0060	electrode	0.0092
Topic 16	**score**	**Topic 17**	**score**	**Topic 18**	**score**
substrate	0.0405	layer	0.0515	semiconductor layer	0.0258
surface	0.0344	chip	0.0231	light emitting element	0.0189
wafer	0.0226	p-type layer	0.0164	electrode	0.0179
gallium	0.0200	sapphire substrate	0.0159	light emitting diode	0.0136
laser beam	0.0061	n-type layer	0.0148	compound semiconductor	0.0097

Topic 19	score	Topic 20	score
substrate	0.0370	layer	0.0258
gallium	0.0272	active region	0.0152
manufacturing	0.0263	device	0.0138
surface	0.0175	first layer	0.0138
thin film	0.0152	second layer	0.0120

B. Research Topics Visualization

Based on LDA model, the metric for terms and topics was measured and used to calculate the similarities between terms. A visualization map was constructed by applying Multidimensional Scaling to the similarities [6]. 20 topics in the GaN field were visualized, as shown in Figure 1. The threshold value for terms showed in the map was 0.001 in this case.

IV. R&D FOCUS EVOLUTING

The metric θ of topics and documents was used to find the topic contributing the most to every document. $\theta_{i,j}$ can reveal the degree to which topic i is referred to in the document j, (1). p(topic=i | θ) according to Dirichlet distribution ($\theta_{i,j} \geq 0, \sum_{i} \theta_{i,j} = 1$) [7]. The most contributed topic was assigned for every document in this case.

$$\theta_{m\times k} = \begin{matrix} & topic_0 & topic_1 & \dots & topic_k & \\ \left[\begin{matrix} \\ \\ \\ \\ \end{matrix}\right. & \begin{matrix}\theta_{0,0} \\ \theta_{1,0} \\ \vdots \\ \theta_{m,0}\end{matrix} & \begin{matrix}\theta_{0,1} \\ \theta_{1,1} \\ \\ \theta_{m,1}\end{matrix} & \begin{matrix}\cdots \\ \cdots \\ \ddots \\ \cdots\end{matrix} & \begin{matrix}\theta_{0,k} \\ \theta_{1,0} \\ \vdots \\ \theta_{m,k}\end{matrix} & \left.\begin{matrix} \\ \\ \\ \\ \end{matrix}\right] \begin{matrix}doc_0 \\ doc_1 \\ \vdots \\ doc_k\end{matrix} \end{matrix} \quad (1)$$

The evolution of R&D focus through new terms emerging in every year was observed. All documents were grouped by year, and terms in a year's documents were counted. $Terms_y$ means terms in year. Then, (2) was used to extract new emerging terms in year y, E_y , ranked by sum of TF-IDF scores.

$$E_y = Terms_y - \sum_{n=y0}^{y-1} Terms_n. \quad (2)$$

In practice, the top technical terms are ranked and identified by term frequency and TF-IDF value. But there are a large number of high frequency general terms by term frequency rank while the technical terms obtained by TF-IDF are more meaningful. Based on (2), new emerging terms were counted from 2011 to 2017 every year in GaN field, as shown in Figure 2.

V. CONCLUSIONS AND FUTURE WORK

The analysis model proposed in this paper gives an efficient way to find technology focus evolution from a large scale text data, such as patent information in this case. Compared with topic level analysis, the tech evolution provides a breakthrough point for finer granularity analyzing to discover hot tech researches on a timescale which could be a clue for finding more information about these tech focuses. In the future, we will continue to optimize the analysis model in practice, especially the processing of synonyms.

REFERENCES

[1] T. L. Griffiths and M. Steyvers, "Finding scientific topics," PNAS, vol. 101, pp. 5228-5235, 2004.

[2] D. Choi, B. Song. "Exploring Technological Trends in Logistics: Topic Modeling-Based Patent Analysis," Sustainability, vol. 10, pp. 2810-2835, 2018.

[3] X. C. Gong and X. Y. An, "A Research of Topic Splitting and Merging Detecting in the Medical Field Based on the LDA Model," Library and Information Service, vol. 61, pp. 64-74, 2017.

[4] J. B. Qu and S. Y. Ou, "Analyzing Topic Evolution with Topic Filtering and Relevance". Data Analysis and Knowledge Discovery, vol. 2, pp. 64-75, 2018.

[5] D. Bourigault, "Surface Grammatical Analysis for the Extraction of Terminological Noun Phrases," In Proc. of COLING the 14th conference on Computational linguistics, pp. 977-981, 1992.

[6] L. Wang, L. X. Zou and X. W. Liu, "Research of Correlation Information Mining and Visualizing Based on the LAD model," Data Analysis and Knowledge Discovery, vol. 2, pp. 98-106, 2018.

[7] D. M. Blei, A. Y. Ng and M. I. Jordan, "Latent Dirichlet allocation," Journal of Machine Learning Research. vol. 3, pp. 993-1022, 2003.

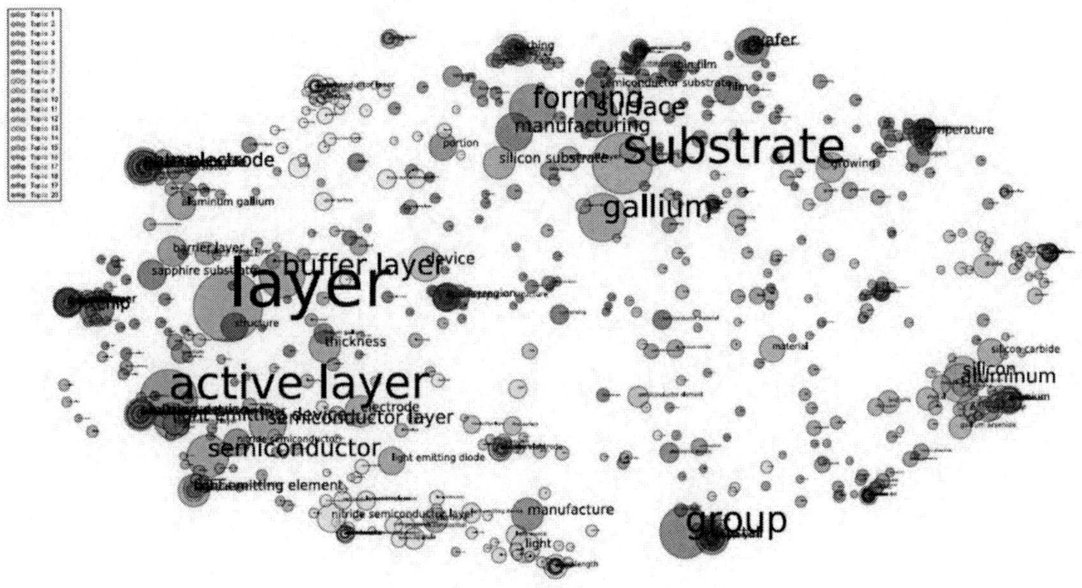

Figure 1. Visualization of GaN research topics

Figure 2. GaN Tech evolution based on new terms from 2011 to 2017

A Feature Extraction Framework for Time Series Analysis

An Application for EEG Signal Processing for Epileptic Seizures Detection

Angelo Martone, Gaetano Zazzaro
Italian Aerospace Research Centre, CIRA
Capua (CE), Italy
e-mail: {a.martone, g.zazzaro}@cira.it

Luigi Pavone
Neuromed, IRCCS
Pozzilli (IS), Italy
e-mail: bioingegneria@neuromed.it

Abstract—**With the raise of smart sensors and of the Internet of Things paradigm, there is an increasing demand for performing Data Mining tasks (classification, clustering, outlier detection, etc.) on data stream produced by these inter-connected devices. In particular, Data Mining for time series has gained a relevant importance in the last decade. For these temporal data, feature extraction can be performed using various algorithms and decomposition techniques for time series analysis. In addition, features can also be obtained by sequence comparison techniques, such as dynamic time warping or other measures of similarity. For these reasons, we have designed and implemented a multipurpose and extendable tool for window-based feature extraction from time series data. This paper describes the architecture of the designed tool, named Training Builder, and the current version of its multi-language implementation, which focuses on time series feature extraction, parametric windowing task and data pre-processing. The framework has been applied in the neurological domain where very good results have been achieved for epileptic seizures detection; the case study shows how the Training Builder tool may be very helpful for the next Data Mining tasks.**

Keywords-data mining; time series analysis; feature extraction; sliding window; similarity measures; pre-processing.

I. INTRODUCTION

In many application fields, such as production lines in factories or stock quotes analysis, it is quite usual to create and process high amounts of data at high rates. Such continuous data flows with unknown size and end are called data streams [1]. When elements of a data stream have a temporal ordering, we talk about time series data. Today, the primary source of data streams are smart sensors that are ubiquitous devices crucial for a multitude of monitoring applications. Important examples are weather observation and environment monitoring in general, health monitoring, Radio-Frequency IDentification (RFID) monitoring, or road monitoring. There are several important tasks that have to be considered when dealing with time series data; among these are: signal pre-processing transformation, time-based windowing and feature extraction process. All these different tasks are usually separately implemented in the freely available tools, see Section II, and it is often hard to combine them to achieve the desired workflow. Being motivated by this observation, we have designed and developed a multipurpose and extensible tool called Training Builder, with the aim of supporting Data Mining process on time series data, implementing data representations, similarity measures and pre-processing modules. It also makes possible to easily change some existing or to add new concrete implementation of any module or algorithm. We have implemented many features and similarity measures, and we have performed a set of experiments to validate their advantages.

In Section II, we examine some time series data analysis tools that exist in the literature. In Section III, we present time series analysis general outlines, including main definitions, its scope and its role in Data Mining (DM). In Section IV, the Training Builder Tool is presented, including the main definitions, feature extraction process, and Graphical User Interface (GUI). In Section V, we show how the application has been applied to a case study in neurological domain. Finally, in Section VI, our general considerations and future works are shown.

II. RELATED WORK

Many tools and applications deal with time series data, each of which differs by the type of approach.

There is a category of tools specialized in the implementation of DM algorithms, such as Waikato Environment for Knowledge Analysis (WEKA) [2] and RapidMiner [3]. WEKA tool supports a great number of DM and machine learning techniques, including data pre-processing, classification, regression and visualization. However, WEKA is a general-purpose DM library, not specialised for time series. Instead, the time series support within WEKA is based on Massive Online Analysis (MOA) [3] tool, which is an open source framework for data stream mining, with a very active growing community. It includes a collection of machine learning algorithms (classification, regression, clustering, outlier detection, etc.) and tools for evaluation. Another system similar to WEKA is RapidMiner. It is also an open source (only the Community Edition) collection of data-mining and machine-learning techniques. RapidMiner has a very sophisticated graphical user interface, and it is also extensible with the user's implementations. Time series support is demanded to the Time Series Extension package that is in alpha version at this moment.

In addition, there are several tools specialised for monitoring and visualisation of time series. Kibana [5] is an open source analytics and visualization platform designed to work with Elasticsearch [6]. It enables near real-time analysis and visualization of streaming data. It allows interactive data exploration, supports cross filtering and provides multiple chart types, such as bar chart, line and scatter plots, histograms, pie charts, and maps. It is open source and has a number of plug-in extensions that can further enhance its functionality. Grafana [6] is another open source visualization tool that can be used on the top of a variety of different data stores, especially on the top of Time Series DataBases (TSDB), such as OpenTSDB [8] and KairosDB [9].

Lastly, there are several massive data stream processing frameworks specialized in manipulation of time series data produced at high rate and with a large volume, such as Apache Spark [10] and Apache Flink [11]. Apache Spark is a batch-processing framework with stream processing capabilities. Built using many of the same principles of Hadoop's MapReduce engine, Spark focuses primarily on speeding up batch processing workloads by offering full in-memory computation and processing optimization. Spark has a specific module, Spark Streaming, which supplies stream processing capabilities, making use of the so-called micro-batches. Apache Flink is a stream processing framework that can also handle batch tasks. It considers batches as data streams with finite boundaries, and thus treats batch processing as a subset of stream processing. This stream-first approach has been called the Kappa architecture [12], in contrast to the more widely known Lambda architecture [13].

Currently, however, there is no freely available standalone system or framework that, at the same time, provides efficient implementations of features extraction process and data pre-processing techniques for time series data and supports the necessary concepts of data representation, similarity measures and signal filtering tasks. In this paper, we propose a software application that tries to combine all the different aforementioned approaches (algorithms, visualization, storage, and parallel/distributed computation) in order to facilitate the user in the DM step.

The implemented tool, called Training Builder, covers all the data preparation tasks, ranging from the signal pre-processing step to the data labeling one, by using the sliding window paradigm and the features calculation algorithms, enriched by functionalities of data storage and data visualization. Training Builder has also been developed to be as extensible as possible, allowing to easily add algorithms for feature calculation to the existing core implementation, thanks to an extremely flexible and modular architecture, and the algorithms can be developed with different programming languages. Lastly, a user-friendly and Web-oriented GUI allows the user to select the temporal parameters and the features to be extracted from the input time series and, showing the charts of features over time, it allows to quickly evaluate and optimize the temporal parameters by mutual comparisons.

III. TIME SERIES ANALYSIS & MINING

Time series analysis is composed of methods that attempt to extract meaningful statistics and other characteristics from data points, to understand the underlying context, and to make forecasts. Time series data are popular in many applications, such as stock market analysis, process control, observation of natural phenomena, scientific and engineering experiments, medical treatments, etc. Therefore, in the last decade, there has been increased interest in querying and mining such data. The purpose of time series mining is to try to extract all meaningful knowledge from the shape of the data. Even if humans have a natural capacity to perform these tasks, it remains a complex problem for computers. In recent years, many efforts have been made to find new methodologies for different time series mining [14] task types including indexing, classification, clustering, prediction, segmentation, anomaly detection, motif discovery, etc.

There are several important concepts that should be taken into account when dealing with time series: pre-processing transformation, time-based parametric windowing, feature extraction, and visualization.

A. Pre-Processing Transformation

"Raw" time series usually contain some distortions, which could be consequences of bad measurements or just a property of the underlying process that generated the time series. The presence of distortions can seriously deteriorate the indexing problem because the distance between two "raw" time series could be very large even though their overall shape is very similar.

The task of the pre-processing transformations is to remove different kinds of distortions. Some of the most common pre-processing tasks are: offset translation, amplitude scaling, removing linear trend, removing noise, etc. [15].

Pre-processing transformations can greatly improve the performance of time series applications by removing different kinds of distortions.

B. Parametric Windowing Technique

Windowing is one of the most frequently used processing methods for data streams. An unbounded stream of data (events) is split into finite sets, or windows, based on specified criteria, such as time. A window can be conceptualized as an in-memory table in which events are added and removed based on a set of policies.

This subsection describes how sliding and tumbling windows work. Both types of windows move across continuous streaming data, splitting the data into finite sets. Finite windows are helpful for operations, such as aggregations, joins, feature extraction, and pattern matching.

1) Tumbling Window

In a tumbling window, tuples are grouped in a single window based on time or count. A tuple belongs to only one window.

For example, consider a time-based tumbling window like the one shown in Fig. 1 with a length of five seconds. The first window (*w1*) contains events that arrived between the zeroth and fifth seconds. The second window (*w2*) contains events that arrived between the fifth and tenth seconds, the third window (*w3*) contains events that arrived between tenth and fifteenth seconds, and finally the fourth window (*w4*) contains events that arrived between fifteenth and twentieth seconds. The tumbling window is evaluated every five seconds, with no overlap between different time windows; each segment represents a distinct time segment.

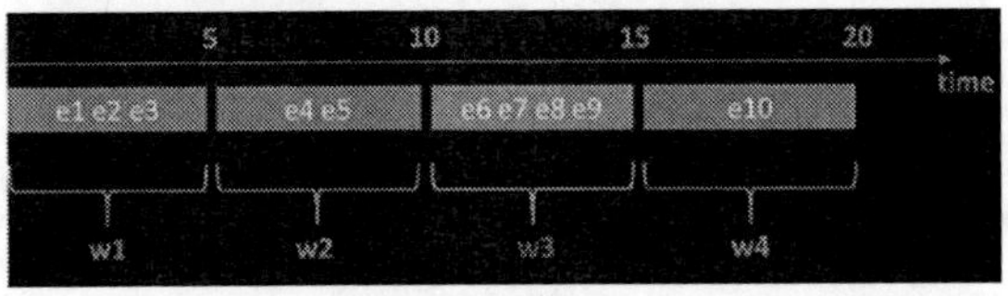

Figure 1. A tumbling windowing process.

This method can be applied, for example, for the computation of the average of a price of a stock over the last five minutes, repeated every five minutes.

2) Sliding Window

In a sliding window, tuples are packed within a window that moves across the stream of data according to a fixed interval. A time-based sliding window with a length of x seconds and a sliding interval of y seconds contains tuples that arrive within an x-second window. The tuples within the window are evaluated every y seconds. Sliding windows can contain overlapping data and the same event can belong to more than one sliding window.

An example is shown in Fig. 2. The first window (*w1*, the green box) contains events occurring between the zeroth and tenth seconds. The second window (*w2*, the orange box) contains events between the fifth and fifteenth seconds. Note that events *e4* through *e5* are in both windows. When window w2 is evaluated at time t = 15 seconds, events *e1*, *e2*, and *e3* are dropped from the event queue.

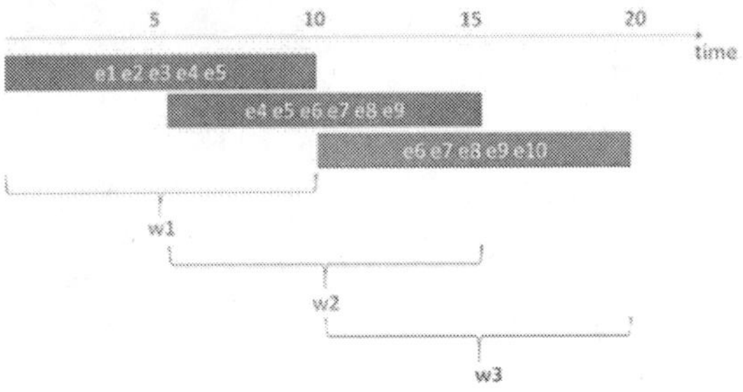

Figure 2. A sliding windowing process.

The time windows w1, w2, w3 contain overlapping data.

C. Features Extraction Task

Feature extraction aims to explain the underlying phenomena of interest from a set of raw data by simplifying the amount of resources required to accurately describe it. In various fields, such as image processing or bio-informatics, raw data are corrupted with undesired variations, or noise, that should be discarded. Thus, feature extraction methods usually consist of a combination of noise removal algorithms (also called de-noising), structure detection, and dimensionality reduction techniques. Generally, an optimal balance is required to be found between fineness and complexity of the extracted features. The desired output should use a minimal amount of resources while being able to accurately describe the underlying phenomena of interest of the data. Once the relevant part of the signal has been extracted, detailed analysis may be conducted, hypotheses may be drawn, and further applications may be considered by the end-user.

Features could be extracted either from one signal (univariate) or from two or more signals (multivariate). In particular, bivariate features are based on a similarity measure that compares two time series objects and returns a value that encodes how similar they are. Distance metrics represent a kind of similarity measures commonly used to define if two time series are similar. Many algorithms are used to compute these metrics, such as Lp distance (Lp) [16], Dynamic Time Warping (DTW) [17], distance based on Longest Common Subsequence (LCSS) [18], Edit Distance (ED) [19], also known as Levenshtein Distance, etc.

D. Data Visualization

Data visualization is a general term that describes any effort to help people understand the significance of data by placing it in a visual context. A graphical visualization of time series could help Data Analyst to better understand time series evolution and to find patterns, correlations or trends.

Usually, a time series is represented by a line graph or a stacked area chart, where the observations are plotted against the corresponding sampling time. A line graph is the simplest way to represent time series data and it uses points connected by lines (also called trend lines). For temporal time series, it represents how the signal changes across time, so how the dependent variable (the signal) changes according to the independent variable (the time).

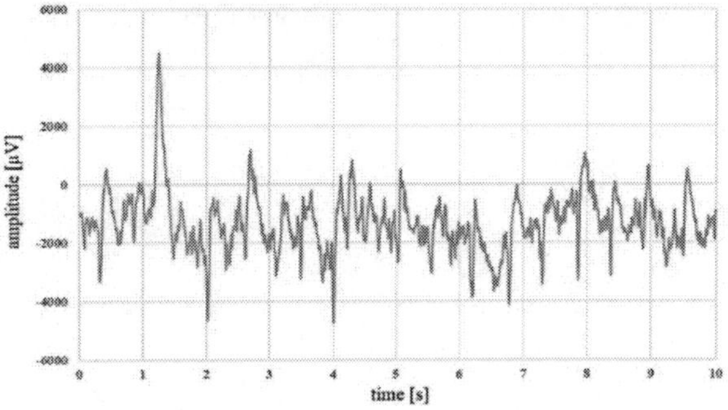

Figure 3. A line graph chart reporting ten seconds of an EEG recording.

The graph in Fig. 3 shows the first ten seconds of an ElectroEncephaloGram (EEG) that measures human brain's electrical activity; along the y-axis is plotted the amplitude of the measured signal in microvolt, while the x-axis has the time in seconds.

IV. Training Builder Tool

The Training Builder is a modular software application for the massive extraction of features from time series, provided as input, by changing of the temporal analysis parameters and the band-pass filters.

The final output of the tool is to create the training sets that will be used as input for the DM techniques. Therefore, each set of training varies depending on:

- Time series (or better the recording of them).
- Temporal analysis parameters: L, R, and S.
- Band-pass filters: [8][12], [13][20], etc.
- Features to be computed (Hjorth Parameters, Statistical Moments, etc.).
- Bivariate calculation method: bivariate algorithms can be used to compute similarity distance between the under examination signal and a "reference" signal.

Each training set consists of a comma-separated values (csv) file, where features are recorded as vectors.

A. Software Architecture and GUI

The software application architecture has been designed following the Client / Server architectural model, in which the Server part is composed of the algorithm for massively extracting features, pre-processing functions, and other support utilities, while the Client part is composed of a browser-based application, responsible for visualizing output results and submitting a form for input selection and validation.

Fig. 4 shows the high-level diagram of the designed software architecture, including the input data sources and the outputs delivered; accordingly, two possible time series data sources are provided:

- Recorded in text format (txt or csv).
- Stored in a TSDB (OpenTSDB or KairosDB).

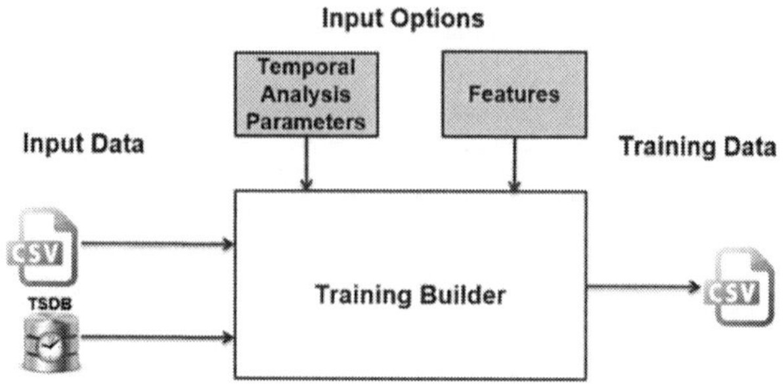

Figure 4. Application logic scheme.

The use of a time series database, instead of formatted files, allows an optimization in the management of time series, as regards their storage and recovery, while ensuring high reliability and availability.

Currently, the application can store and retrieve time series data from the OpenTSDB and KairosDB time series databases, which in turn store data on the NoSQL databases Apache HBase [21] and Apache Cassandra [22], respectively. This double possibility allows the Training Builder to adapt to different software configurations.

In output, instead, the results of the application of features to these time series are provided in csv format. The csv file can be saved by the client or stored on a distributed file system.

Figure 5. Training Builder GUI.

By using the responsive Web-oriented GUI, shown in Fig. 5, the input sources, all the temporal parameters, the bandwidths, and the features can be chosen and selected by the user. A direct interface to the time series visualization browser, provided by the above-mentioned TSDB, is also provided.

The GUI can be divided into four functional blocks, as highlighted by numbered circles in Fig. 5. The first block enables user to select the time series that has to be analysed, selecting a local csv file or choosing a stored time series in the TSDB. In the second block, the user can specify the time series sampling rate and can select the bandwidth intervals. In the third block, the temporal analysis parameters are listed (see Section IV.D). In the fourth block, the user can select the univariate and bivariate features to be computed from the selected time series data (see Section IV.E) and the calculation methods useful to extract the bivariate ones (see Section IV.F for deeper details). Lastly, a set of buttons allows the following operations:

- Process: starts data analysis process.
- Stop: stops the running computation.
- Show Graph Charts: shows the plot charts of the raw data and filtered time series (an example is reported in Fig. 7) in a separate browser window.

This client component was developed using the jQuery JavaScript library [20]; in particular, it was used to manipulate the Document Object Model (DOM) interface of the Hyper Text Markup Language (HTML) page and for asynchronous communications with the Server part, by using Asynchronous JavaScript and XML (AJAX) technology.

The Server component is instead divided into two layers:

- The Application Layer, which includes the logic that implements the analysis algorithms and how they are used for the massive extraction of the features, according to the chosen temporal parameters and other user selected inputs.
- The Data Layer, which is represented by the time series database chosen (OpenTSDB and KairosDB) or text/csv files.

Each of these layers could be instantiated on a dedicated workstation improving the overall performances of the software application.

Furthermore, Training Builder has been developed to be as extensible as possible, with the aim of being able to execute algorithms for feature computation developed with different programming languages; currently Java, C/C++ and Matlab are natively supported, but compatibility with other languages like R and Python, which are widely used for time series analysis tasks, can be easily configured. This capability is achieved thanks to Java Native Interface (JNI) and Service Provider Interface technologies (SPI) offered by Java Virtual Machine (JVM).

B. Core System Funcionalities

The core of the system consists of a set of algorithms for features implementation and routines for the definition of temporal analysis parameters. The choice of which parameters and which features to apply to the input files is delegated to the user and is simplified through a Web-oriented graphical user interface. The application is also compliant with the architectural pattern Representational State Transfer (REST) [23]: using a stateless protocol and standard operations, REST systems provide high performance, reliability, and scalability, reusing components that can be managed and updated without affecting the system as a whole, even while it is running. The REST APIs, which act as wrappers for the developed algorithms, can be called as services from external applications; in this way, for example, the application can be integrated into existing software platforms or recalled by other remote Web services. The Web application can be run on any standard Java Application Server; for our tests Apache Tomcat [24] has been used, because it is the most widespread and used in the Open Source community.

The algorithmic component (that is, the component that contains the features algorithms) has been coded using Java, Matlab and C programming languages. The choice of the language to be used is related to the complexity of the algorithm (for example, in Matlab it is much easier to work on matrices and vectors) and the availability of built-in functions that can simplify the coding of the algorithm itself. Consider, for example, the Log-Energy Entropy feature, which requires the wavelet transform of the input signal: its implementation is easier in Matlab environment as it provides a series of utility functions to obtain the wavelet transform of a signal (both discrete and continuous).

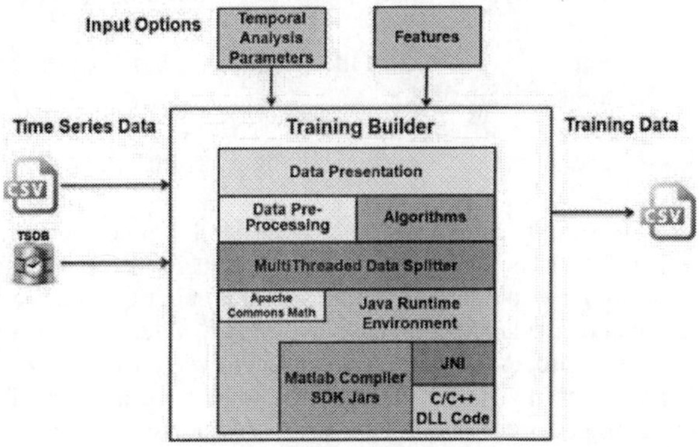

Figure 6. Application components scheme.

In order to execute algorithms implemented in Matlab environment, a series of utility classes were developed in Java (using the Matlab Compiler SDK tool), which are able to interoperate with the Matlab environment through the Matlab Runtime [25]. The Matlab Runtime is a standalone set of shared libraries that allows running applications compiled by Matlab or Matlab components on computers where Matlab is not installed. The Matlab Runtime behaves very similar to a JVM, allowing code portability on Windows, Linux and Mac machines. Where possible, the equivalent C code of the algorithm developed in Matlab was generated automatically using the Matlab Coder toolbox. This eliminates the dependency on the Matlab Runtime, but the corresponding library must be generated according to the host Operating System (DLL for Windows, Shared Object for Linux). Unfortunately, this operation is not always supported; in fact, in the case of Log-Energy Entropy this was not possible because the wavelet functions cannot be generated in C, so the code requires the Matlab Runtime to be installed on the host machine. The Multithreaded Data Splitter component, shown in purple in Fig. 6, is responsible of splitting the dataset to be analysed, into sub-blocks of data, in order to exploit the multithreading capabilities of modern processors, parallelizing the execution of the program and consequently increasing its performance. The input to the component can be one or more files to be analysed or even one or more streams retrieved from the time series database; both types of input are converted into a standard internal format so, for simplicity, we will now use the generic term source to indicate one of the two input types. The component implements an algorithm to define the number of threads to be used and then calculates how to split the data provided by the source between the different threads. Indicating with *MaxNumThread* the number of threads manageable by the processor and *NumSources* the number of sources to be analysed, the algorithm follows these steps:

1. One thread is reserved for each source to be analysed (at most equal to MaxNumThread).
2. Each of the threads of the ith source can in turn launch a number of secondary threads equal to:

$$NumThread_i = MaxNumThread / NumSources \quad (1)$$

3. For each jth thread of the ith source, a block of data is assigned equal to:

$$DataBlock_{ji} = SourceDataLength / NumThread_i \quad (2)$$

For example, suppose you have an Intel™ processor with 8 cores and each core can handle 2 threads using Hyper-Threading technology, obtaining a total number of 16 threads that can be managed simultaneously (*MaxNumThread*); if we wanted to process 4 sources in parallel (*NumSources*) of data length equal to 10000 values, we would have a thread for each single source (1). Each source is then associated with a number of threads ($NumThread_i$) equal to 16/4 = 4. Each of these four threads is assigned a portion of data equal to 10000/4 = 2500 values (2).

The Java implementation of this component makes use of the concurrency APIs, where the Executor framework as a layer of higher level in thread management has been implemented. Executors replace the direct execution mode of threads, allowing the implementation of asynchronous tasks and thread pools. Each thread inside the pool is reusable: an Executor does not autonomously terminate its execution but waits for the execution of new tasks. In our tests, we have seen an almost linear performance speedup, by increasing the number of threads used.

C. Signal Pre-Processing

Data pre-processing is made up of a set of techniques able to transform the raw data into some meaningful and understandable format. It is advisable to identify the main frequency components of a signal in order to eliminate the so-called out-of-band noise. The choice of the frequency bands to be used for processing the signals under examination also depends on the type of the signal and on the frequency at which it was acquired. The upper limit is dictated by the sampling frequency (as stated by the Nyquist–Shannon sampling theorem). The bandpass filters, encapsulated in the yellow block of Fig. 6, have been implemented in the Matlab environment by using the Fast Fourier Transform (FFT) function.

D. Parametric Windowing

Parametric Windowing in Training Builder is achieved by using three temporal analysis parameters:

- *L*: it represents the length of the signal to be analysed, expressed in seconds [s].
- *S*: it represents the slippage of the signal to be analysed (i.e., how often the algorithm is applied), expressed in seconds [s].
- *R*: it represents the forecast radius, expressed in seconds [s].

If the sliding step size *S* is smaller than the window size *L*, the windows overlap, while if $S = L$ we get a tumbling window. *R* parameter is helpful to tag each computed feature with a target class (this is helpful for the next DM).

E. Implemented Features

The Algorithms green block, in Fig. 6, is the component responsible of features algorithms computation.

TABLE I. COMPUTED FEATURES ALGORITHMS

Id	*Feature Name*	*Code*	*UB*	*Coding*
1	Mean	SM1	U	Java
2	Standard Deviation	SM2	U	Java
3	Variance	SM3	U	Java
4	Skewness	SM4	U	Java
5	Kurtosis	SM5	U	Java
6	Hjorth Mobility	HP1	U	Java
7	Hjorth Complexity	HP2	U	Java
8	Shannon Entropy	EB1	U	Java
9	Log-Energy Entropy	EB2	U	Matlab
10	Kolmogorov Complexity	CB1	U	Matlab/C
11	Upper Limit Lempel-Ziv Complexity	CB2	U	Matlab/C
12	Lower Limit Lempel-Ziv Complexity	CB3	U	Matlab/C
13	Peak Displacement	SE1	U	Java
14	Predominant Period	SE2	U	Java
15	Averaged Period	SE3	U	Java
16	Squared Grade	SE4	U	Java
17	Squared Time to Peak	SE5	U	Java
18	Inverted Time to Peak	SE6	U	Java
19	Conditional Entropy	MC1	B	Java
20	Joint Entropy	MC2	B	Java
21	Mutual Information	MC3	B	Java
22	Cross Correlation Index	MC4	B	Java
23	Euclidean Distance	DB1	B	Java
24	Levenshtein Distance	DB2	B	Java
25	Dynamic Time Warping	DB3	B	Java
26	Longest Common Sub-Sequence	DB4	B	Java

Currently, 26 algorithms have been implemented, that could be divided into 7 classes and can be of Univariate (U) or Bivariate type (B):

- SM: Statistical Moments.
- HP: Hjorth Parameters.
- EB: Entropy Based.
- CB: Complexity Based.
- SE: Seismic Evaluators.
- MC: Mutual Conditioned.
- DB: Distance Based.

In Table I, a list of all implemented features is reported, and it is also specified with which programming language the algorithm has been coded.

A description of the more relevant implemented features is reported below.

1) Statistical Moments

In mathematics, a moment is a specific quantitative measure of the shape of a function. In our framework, the first four statistical moments have been calculated, plus standard deviation measure. All algorithms where developed in Java by using the Apache Commons Math library [26].

2) Hjorth's parameters

Hjorth's parameters (normalized slope descriptors) of mobility and complexity [27] quantify the root-mean-square frequency and the root-mean-square frequency spread of a given signal, respectively.

3) Shannon Entropy

In Information Theory, the Shannon's Entropy represents the average amount of information produced by a stochastic source of data. Formally, it is defined as the expected value of self-information. The latter represents the information contained in a given event x, emitted by the source X and it is defined as follows:

$$I(x) = -\log_2 P(x) \qquad (3)$$

Thus, the entropy of a source X turns out to be:

$$H(X) = E[I(X)] = E[-\log_2 P(x)] \qquad (4)$$

where $P(X)$ is a probability mass function for a discrete random variable X.

4) Log-Energy Entropy

The Log-Energy Entropy is a feature closely related to Shannon's Entropy and to Wavelet Transform. In fact, after an appropriate wavelet decomposition, it is possible to calculate the Log-Energy Entropy by using the following relation:

$$E(s) = \sum_{i=1} \log_2 (s_i^2) \qquad (5)$$

where s_i are the N coefficients of the wavelet transform for the signal s emitted.

5) Kolmogorov Complexity

In Algorithmic Information Theory, the Kolmogorov Complexity of an object, such as a piece of text, is the length of the shortest computer program (in a predetermined programming language) that produces the object as output. It is a measure of the computational resources needed to specify the object and it is also known as descriptive complexity.

6) Lempel-Ziv Complexity

The Lempel-Ziv Complexity of a given finite binary sequence is an index associated with the number of sub-sequences that can be identified. In particular, this process can take place through methods that tend to highlight the greater or lesser complexity of the given sequence. Therefore, taking into account the two extremes, it is possible to calculate those that are interpreted as the upper and lower limit of this index.

7) Seismic Evaluators

The seismic evaluators have been calculated by considering [28] and [29] because there is an analogy between earthquakes and epileptic seizures.

8) Dynamic Time Warping

Dynamic Time Warping is a technique that uses dynamic programming to compare two sequences of different lengths and allows non-linear alignments, one-to-many, or vice versa, thanks to a temporal distortion. A nonlinear (elastic) alignment produces a more intuitive measure of similarity and favours those cases in which the sequences are similar but locally out of phase.

F. Bivariate Features Calculation Methods

Bivariate algorithms have been used to compute similarity distance between the under examination signal and a "reference" signal. This reference signal could be of three different types:

- W.r.t. Previous L: with respect to the same signal taken at a previous L interval.
- W.r.t. Zero: with respect to the zero constant signal.
- W.r.t. Different Synchronous Signal: with respect to a synchronous signal happening in the same instant but originated from a different positioning.

V. CASE STUDY IN NEUROLOGICAL DOMAIN

Epilepsy is a neurological disorder characterized by recurrent seizures caused by abnormal electrical discharges from the brain cells, which extremely affect patient quality of life. The worldwide recognized standard for epilepsy monitoring and diagnosing is ElectroEncephaloGram (EEG) recorded from scalp or intracranially (iEEG). The former is the most commonly used ambulatory method, mainly due to its low invasiveness, while the latter is mainly used to help patients in which classical EEG monitoring is not able to identify epileptic area. A lot of interest there is in finding automated seizure detection methods from EEG/iEEG, to help clinicians to identify seizures on EEG/iEEG recordings and also to embed them in closed-loop systems for epilepsy control. Feature extraction method for epileptic EEG/iEEG plays a crucial role in detection algorithms, since it seriously affects the performance of these algorithms.

A. *Training Builder on Working*

We used Training Builder to analyse iEEG signals for the detection of epileptic seizures. In particular, by analysing the fraction of the iEEG recordings immediately preceding the beginning of the epileptic seizure (PreIctal recordings) and the ones belonging to the seizure itself (Ictal recordings), a classifier is trained in order to determine the anomalous signals, using the numerous computed predictive features.

A public iEEG dataset, the Freiburg Seizure Prediction EEG database (FSPEEG) [30], was used for evaluating the classification performance of extracted features. The database contains iEEG recordings from 21 patients with medically intractable epilepsy. Recordings were made by means of grids, strips, and depth electrodes, and acquired with a 128 channel system at 256 Hz sampling rate. Six iEEG channels were selected by certified epileptologists, three from focal electrodes (InFokus channels), located near to the region where the seizures occurred and three from extra focal electrodes (OutFokus channels), located in areas far from the seizure focus. In our test, we examined twelve recordings of one patient (number 16): five containing seizures (Ictal) and seven without seizures (PreIctal), were observed.

In order to detect the beginning of the epileptic seizure within the iEEG signals, a binary classifier can be trained starting from the training set formed by the computed features and whose target class is *ActualYN*, which assumes the values {*YES*, *NO*}: *YES* if we are in Ictal phase, *NO* otherwise.

B. *iEEG Pre-Processing*

The iEEG signal from each InFokus/OutFokus electrode was filtered through six different frequency bands, 8-12 Hz, 13-20 Hz, 21-30 Hz, 30-45 Hz, 40-70 Hz and 70-120 Hz using band-pass filter, thus obtaining six signals. The upper limit of 120 Hz is dictated by the sampling frequency with which the iEEG signal was acquired at 256 Hz. Moreover, a notch filter at 50 Hz, to minimize power line interferences, has been used.

C. *Feature Extraction Process*

The first step before feature extraction is the selection of the window size L and the sliding step S for the sliding window calculation task. R parameter is used to select the value of the *ActualYN* target class.

TABLE II. TEMPORAL PARAMETER VALUES

L	*R*	*S*
5 [s]	0 [s]	1 [s]

For this case study, we selected temporal parameter values (in seconds) as listed in Table II; with $S < L$ we had choose an overlapped window and we set $R = 0$ because we wanted to detect the onset of the epileptic seizure.

For this case study, we decided to compute all features provided by the Training Builder tool for all possible combination of electrodes, bandwidths and type of reference signal; the size of the final feature dataset is then:

$$(a + b * c + b * d) * e * f \qquad (6)$$

where a are the univariate features, b the bivariate features, c bivariate modality calculation, d the type of reference signal, e the bandwidths and f the electrodes.

TABLE III. FEATURE DATASET VARIABLES VALUE

a	*b*	*c*	*d*	*e*	*f*
18	8	3	3	6	6

In this case study, we have 2376 variables, as reported in Table III.

Training Builder tool tags every extracted vector of features with the corresponding value of the target class *ActualYN*.

D. *iEEG Data Visualization*

Training Builder tool provides also a graphical user interface to visualize and analyse the input time series. This is achieved using the time series visual editors that both OpenTSDB and KairosDB provide. Otherwise, Grafana can be used, which deals well with the two TSDB. In this case study, the GUI made available by KairosDB has been used.

In Fig. 7, the first 30 seconds of the patient's registration 001 have been displayed, recorded from the electrode 1 and filtered in the band [13,20] Hz, for a total of 7680 samples (considering the sampling freq. of 256 Hz).

These charts are also very useful for visually detecting the various seizures phases.

E. *Modeling*

In the classification step, we hypothesized that the different features extracted over time can be separated into two classes corresponding to two different cerebral states (Ictal and PreIctal).

By analysing the fraction of PreIctal and Ictal recordings, a classifier model has been trained in order to determine the anomalous signals, using the calculated features. We chose as classifier a multilayer neural network (Multilayer Perceptron) with 20 hidden layers (H = 20). From our tests, it is able to correctly classify the 99.27% of records, including 95% of records of the *YES* class.

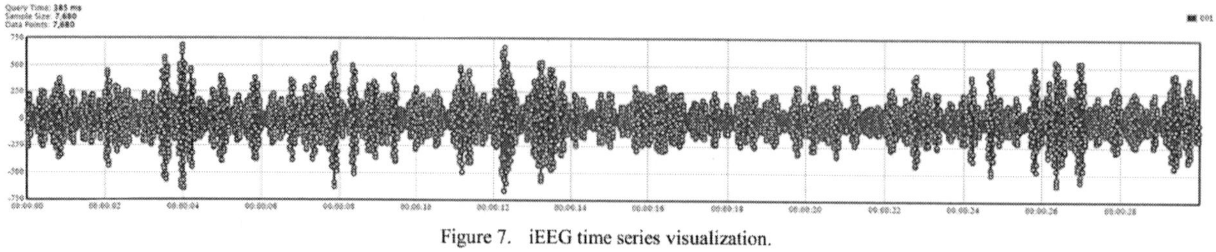

Figure 7. iEEG time series visualization.

To get further details of the Modeling phase of DM process and additional interesting methods and results, you can see [31], where Support Vector Machines have been trained in order to detect epileptic seizures in the iEEG signals.

VI. Conclusions and Future Works

In this work, we proposed a time-based windowed framework for time series analysis that allows Data Analysts to easily set all different combination of temporal parametric values, bandwidth intervals, and features to extract from a time series. By using a user-friendly software application, we tested a case study in the neurological domain, in order to understand how this approach helps to analyse the dataset, to optimize the feature extraction task and to help the following modelling task of the target dataset, by applying the sliding window paradigm.

As future works, we are going to integrate in our tool some representation techniques that can reduce the dimensionality of time series. These techniques have been proven to limit time and memory consuming, especially when there is a need to compute a similarity distance between time series. Moreover, in the future studies, we are going to use one of the massive data stream processing frameworks, mentioned in Section II.

Acknowledgment

The authors would mention the Big Data Facility project, funded by the Italian Aerospace Research Program (PRORA), in which the tool has been designed and developed.

References

[1] S. Geisler, "Data Stream Management Systems," In: Data Exchange, Information, and Streams, 2013.

[2] M. Hall et al., "The WEKA Data Mining Software: An Update," SIGKDD Explorations, vol. 11, no 1, pp. 10–18, 2009.

[3] M. Hofmann and R. Klinkenberg, "RapidMiner: Data Mining Use Cases and Business Analytics Applications," Chapman & Hall/CRC Data Mining and Knowledge Discovery Series, CRC Press, October 25, 2013.

[4] A. Bifet, G. Holmes, R. Kirkby, and B. Pfahringer, "MOA: Massive Online Analysis," Journal of Machine Learning Research, vol. 11, pp. 1601–1604, 2010.

[5] *Kibana: Explore, Visualize, Discover Data*. [Online]. Available from: https://www.elastic.co/products/kibana, 2019.01.22.

[6] *Open Source Search & Analytics Elasticsearch*. [Online]. Available from: https://www.elastic.co, 2019.01.22.

[7] *Grafana - The open platform for analytics and monitoring*. [Online]. Available from: https://grafana.com, 2019.01.22.

[8] *OpenTSDB, The Scalable Time Series Database*. [Online]. Available from: http://opentsdb.net, 2019.01.22.

[9] *KairosDB, Fast Time Series Database on Cassandra*. [Online]. Available from: https://kairosdb.github.io, 2019.01.22.

[10] M. Zaharia, "An Architecture for Fast and General Data Processing on Large Clusters," PhD Dissertation, 2013.

[11] P. Carbone et al., "Apache Flink: Stream and Batch Processing in a Single Engine," Bulletin of the IEEE Computer Society Technical Committee on Data Engineering, vol. 36, no. 4, pp. 28–38, 2015.

[12] J. Kreps, *Questioning the Lambda Architecture*. [Online]. Available from: https://www.oreilly.com/ideas/questioning-the-lambda-architecture, 2019.01.22.

[13] N. Marz and J. Warren, "Big Data: Principles and best practices of scalable realtime data systems," Manning Publications, 2013.

[14] P. Esling and C. Agon, "Time-series data mining," ACM Computing Surveys (CSUR), vol. 45, no. 1, 2012.

[15] E. Keogh and M. Pazzani, "Relevance Feedback Retrieval of Time Series Data," Proc. 22nd Annual International ACM-SIGIR Conference on Research and Development in Information Retrieval, pp. 183–190, 1999.

[16] R. Agrawal, C. Faloutsos, and A. N. Swami, "Efficient similarity search in sequence databases," Proc. 4th Int. Conf. of Foundations of Data Organization and Algorithms, pp. 69–84, 1993.

[17] D. Berndt and J. Clifford, "Using dynamic time warping to find patterns in time series," Proc. of the 3rd Int. Conf. on Knowledge Discovery and Data Mining, pp 359-370, 1994.

[18] M. Vlachos, D. Gunopulos, and G. Kollios, "Discovering similar multidimensional trajectories," In: ICDE, pp. 673–684, 2002.

[19] R. A. Wagner and M. J. Fischer, "The string-to-string correction problem," Journal of the ACM, vol. 21, no. 1, pp. 168–173, 1974.

[20] *jQuery*. [Online]. Available from: https://jquery.com/, 2019.01.22.

[21] *Apache HBase*. [Online]. Available from: https://hbase.apache.org, 2019.01.22.

[22] *Apache Cassandra*. [Online]. Available from: http://cassandra.apache.org, 2019.01.22.

[23] R. T. Fielding and R. N. Taylor, "Principled design of the modern Web architecture", ACM Transactions on Internet Technology, vol. 2, no. 2, pp. 115–150, 2002.

[24] *Apache Tomcat*. [Online]. Available from: http://tomcat.apache.org, 2019.01.22.

[25] *MATLAB Runtime, Run compiled MATLAB applications or components without installing MATLAB*. [Online]. Available from: https://www.mathworks.com/products/compiler/matlab-runtime.html, 2019.01.22.

[26] *Commons Math: The Apache Commons Mathematics Library*. [Online]. Available from: http://commons.apache.org/proper/commons-math, 2019.01.22.

[27] B. Hjorth, "EEG analysis based on time domain properties," Electroencephalogr. Clinical Neurophysiology, vol. 29, no. 3, pp. 306–310, 1970.

[28] I. Osorio, H. P. Zaveri, M. G. Frei, and S. Arthurs, "Epilepsy: The Intersection of Neurosciences, Biology, Mathematics, Engineering, and Physics," in Rationales for Analogy between Earthquakes, Financial Crashes, and Epileptic Seizures, CRC Press, Taylor & Francis Group, 2011.

[29] G. Zazzaro, F. M. Pisano, and G. Romano, "Bayesian Networks for Earthquake Magnitude Classification in a Early Warning System," International Journal of Environmental, Chemical, Ecological, Geological and Geophysical Engineering, vol. 6, no. 4, 2012.

[30] "The Freiburg Seizure Prediction EEG database," [Online]. Available from: http://epilepsy.uni-freiburg.de/freiburg-seizure-prediction-project/eeg-database, 2019.01.22.

[31] G. Zazzaro et al., "EEG Signal Analysis for Epileptic Seizures Detection by Applying Data Mining Techniques," Internet of Things: Engineering Cyber Physical Human Systems, Elsevier, in press.

Visualizing Autonomous Warehouse Data Streams through User-Centered Design

Raghu Nayyar
Media Technology and Interaction Design
KTH Royal Institute of Technology
Stockholm, Sweden
Email: raghun@kth.se

Didem Gürdür
Department of Machine Design,
KTH Royal Institute of Technology
Stockholm, Sweden
Email: dgurdur@kth.se

Aneta Vulgarakis Feljan
Ericsson Research,
Ericsson
Stockholm, Sweden
Email:
aneta.vulgarakis@ericsson.com

Abstract—**In this paper, we develop and evaluate a dashboard design that visualises a stream of data from different entities involved in autonomous warehouses, as a subset of cyber-physical systems. The dashboard is designed and developed through User-Centered Design (UCD) methodologies based on two iterations of feedback sessions with the stakeholders. During these sessions, semi-structured expert opinion interviews are conducted. The paper discusses the different stages involved in building the proposed dashboard design, the design decisions, the technical aspects of the libraries used, and the results of the feedback sessions towards the end of the project. It also presents the implemented dashboard as a proof of development efforts and explains its different functionalities. The study concludes by evaluating the dashboard through the semi-structured interviews with the respective stakeholders and suggests features for further development.**

Keywords—data visualization; cyber-physical systems; user experience; user-centered design; supply chain; autonomous warehouse; intelligent agents; dashboard design.

I. Introduction

In simple terms, a Cyber-Physical System (CPS) is a system in which different computational and physical processes are being carried out together in order to perform several tasks [1]. These tasks could belong to a wide range of domains, including assisted living, traffic control and safety, advanced automotive systems, distributed robotics defense systems, manufacturing, and smart structures [2][3]. In this paper, we discuss a narrow application of CPS, namely, an automated warehouse.

Traditionally, a warehouse involves four major functions: (1) receiving, (2) storage, (3) order picking, and (4) shipping [3]. Today, there is an ever-increasing demand for a variety of products and shorter response times causing a tremendous emphasis on the ability to establish smooth and efficient logistics operations. These logistic operations are complex and hence produce a lot of data. This data has the potential to be used for further monitoring the complex operations by the stakeholders to understand the current state of the warehouse. Based on this, the stakeholders can analyse several Key Performance Indicators (KPI), including interoperability, knowledge reusability, performance, sustainability, safety, risk, and profitability [4]. Hence, for a smooth functioning and maintenance of these systems, there is a need to gracefully represent these complex data streams in an easy to understand manner.

This study is part of a project, which is called Secure Connected Trustable Things (SCOTT) and focuses on complex logistics use cases. The study explores a dashboard design to best represent the data streams in an automated warehouse to help the stakeholders to monitor the current state of the warehouse. The automated warehouse in question has three levels as follows: (1) Supply Chain level, (2) Warehouse level, (3) Intelligent Agent level [4].

The aim of the project is to address the research question: *What are the suitable visualization techniques that are required to build a dashboard which represents a stream of data from an autonomous warehouse, focusing on KPI such as performance, safety, and sustainability by employing user-centered design methodologies?*

To this end, this report leverages on expert opinion [5] and semi-structured interviews [6] at the onset of the study to understand the needs of stakeholders, gather feedback and suggest new features for further iterations. Section I introduces the concept of CPS and autonomous warehouse, defines the problem statement, the objective of the study, methodology used to achieve that and delimitations of certain procedures and technology used. Section II discusses the previous work done in the field of CPS and autonomous warehouses, different methods to build user friendly dashboards for retailers and smart warehouses. Section III discusses the design process, the initial decisions taken, defining the entities, and building three different dashboard views based of the level of the warehouse. Section IV discusses the metrics for the user study and interviews. Section V explains the results based on the interview feedback. Section VI discusses the results and breaks down similar feedback into three categories. The paper ends with concussion and suggestions for future work in Section VII.

A. Objective

The primary goal of the study is to design and develop a dashboard to answer the defined research question. This dashboard represents a stream of data that comes from the different entities involved in and around an autonomous warehouse which is a fully-automated CPS. These entities include (1) trucks, (2) warehouses, (3) retailers, (4) smart robots, and (5) conveyor belts.

B. Methodology

During the project, the identified stakeholders were interviewed on two stages of the design process. Semi-structured interviewing is a very flexible technique for small-scale research in which detailed structure is left to be worked out during the interview, and the person being interviewed has a fair degree of freedom in what to talk about, how much to say, and how to express it [7]. The feedback session was an informal user study with one stakeholder where a pen-paper prototype was evaluated. Based on the feedback, the final visual design was made which later got converted to a functional prototype. The development was further shaped by feedback from one-to-one semi-structured interviews. Towards the end of the final prototype, a final interview was conducted to get feedback relevant to the next iteration of the dashboard.

To develop this prototype, ReactJS[15], a component-based JavaScript framework was used for the base front-end of the application. It was primarily because of its rendering performance and the ability to break down the application into smaller independent components. D3js[16], the industry standard of data visualization javascript library was used to develop the dashboard prototype. A state machine, Redux, was also introduced to capture the state after every change in the data as an immutable object. This was done to avoid continuously calling the server to make the dashboard more performant. Nivo, a wrapper on top of D3js, was used to make the visualizations. Nivo was preferred because of the flexibility in the layout of the graphs it generates and the data structures are more adaptable unlike libraries like react-d3. ImmutableJS was used to create factories for the entities in the form of records. Fetch was used for the HTTP requests to the server. Postman is used for mocking the back-end API.

C. Delimitations

The project does not involve a real-time data streaming coming from automated warehouse since the research project prototype is still under development. Therefore, there are assumptions made for the structure and properties of the data streams that might change or evolve. Although a very strict data structure is followed and obeyed while building the visualization, there might be performance issues due to the machine learning algorithms. In terms of design, although the dashboard incorporates the UCD approach [7][10], the feedback session is limited to 5 people, considering stakeholders include user experience designers, system engineers and researchers who work on the same project. The dashboard currently incorporates 3 KPI: (1) safety; (2) sustainability; and (3) performance. The scope of the work does not include the identification of the relevant KPI and also does not include the further data integration with the existing or in development CPS. However, the interested reader can learn more about the earlier research conducted as part of the project to identify these KPI [4] and the minimalistic data model for monitoring purpose [8].

II. Background and Related Work

Research in the domain of CPS is driven by several recent factors: (1) the development of low-cost and increased-capability sensors of increasingly smaller form-factor, (2) the availability of low-cost, low-power, high-capacity, small form-factor computing devices, (3) the wireless communication revolution; abundant Internet bandwidth, (4) continuing improvements in energy capacity, alternative energy sources and energy harvesting [1].

As we mentioned before, automated warehouses, an example of CPS, have interactions between different moving parts (or entities) involved in keeping or retrieving different objects present in the warehouse or the interactions of the warehouse with the outside world. The complex nature of these interactions makes it difficult to see the overall activity in and around the warehouse.

In [4], the authors conduct several interviews with experts to identify the important KPIs and stakeholders as a first step. During this work, an example dashboard design is also presented. However, this preliminary study does not include a working prototype.

Furthermore, in [7], (1) safety, (2) sustainability, and (3) performance are chosen as important KPI to monitor through the dashboard.

Safety refers to the level of trust in the warehouse. A collision probability is one example metric used to monitor the safety level in the warehouse.

Performance is related to metrics such as time, goals accomplished by a particular robot or the overall goals of the warehouse.

Sustainability refers to the energy levels of the warehouse. This includes the energy and the battery consumed to perform actions within the warehouse, which is directly correlated to the efficiency of the robots and the warehouse.

Later, a minimalistic data model [8] is presented in the same study through a linked data technologies which promise both consistency and interoperability throughout the CPS in focus.

Other research projects have been working with management dashboards in scenarios specific to retailers and for one of them, the views are split into (1) Management layer, (2) Physical layer, and (3) Agent layer but these layers have not been evaluated by the respective stakeholders [8].

The automated warehouse's smartness is guaranteed by the intelligent agents. These agents are the representations of real components such as robots, smart shelf systems and so on. For this purpose, Soar, a general cognitive architecture, has been a studied as part of the project. It offers demonstrations of individual components, components working in combination, and real-world applications [9]. VISTA is a generic toolkit that allows stakeholders to visualize internal reasoning of these intelligent agents [10]. However, this toolkit is concentrated on the behaviour of the agents, in contrast to, the data streams from the agents.

III. Design Process

A. Initial Design Decisions

In terms of the first design process, the first step was identifying the entities and splitting them into the three levels. Every level was then split into cards and atomic design [11] approach is used to build smaller cards instead of making one big dashboard. Atomic design is a methodology of creating a design system based on creating small components (or atoms) like buttons, inputs, headings, and so on. Later, these components comb are combined to create larger components (or molecules) like forms, button groups and in our case, cards. This approach is chosen for the purpose of making the application as modular as possible.

To make the implementation as light as possible, a highlight boolean variable is included in every entity which enabled to fetch the required data instead of querying all the data. This way, the performance of the prototype is ensured.

The idea of not revealing the entire data set was given prime importance to enhance both experience and performance. Hence, a highlight boolean was introduced in all the entities and only entities set to true by the users were displayed at first and the entire data set was released once requested by clicking the button.

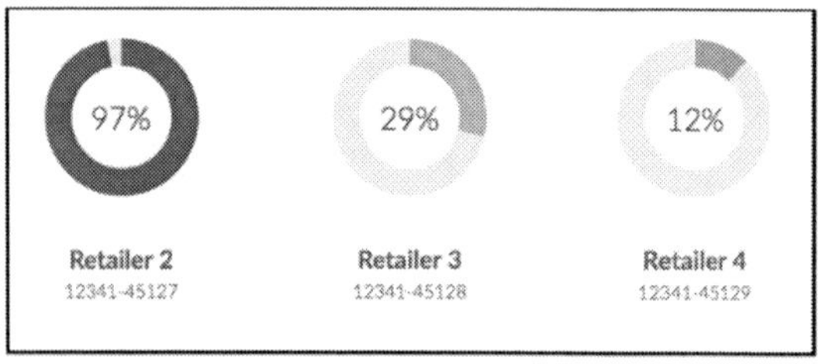

Figure 1. State of the retailers and warehouse on the supply chain level.

The dashboard consisted of a lot of data streams that signify an empty or a full state which could not be expressed only by numbers, hence three colors, based on color selection for highlighting tasks [12] were consistently used to signify negative (full), positive (empty) and in progress space (Figure 1).

As we mentioned before, the warehouse is divided into three levels (supply chain, warehouse, and intelligent agent) and the information for each level is represented by cards. The dashboard is designed in a way that each card owned a separate API request to make all cards independent of each other. Moreover, information text was provided for every card in the form of a tooltip so that the helpful information is only available when needed. These implementation decisions are selected to allow enough resources available for the performative visualizations [13].

B. Defining Entities and Their Records

The following entity records are defined to represent the entire system:

- **Warehouse and Retailers** represent the entire space and consist of a similar data structure composed of an ID (string), highlighted tag (bool), location (geo), the name of the space (string) and the capacity of the space (num). The IDs of these entities are needed for trucks to identify destination and source of their journeys.
- **Robots** of different kinds: (1) arms, (2) conveyor belts, and (3) other retrieval systems are an integral part of the intelligent agent level and warehouse level. Their data stream is comprised of an ID (string), activity, battery and performance indicators with their respective deviation. It also consists of the location ID and the object ID that signifies in which warehouse they are present and the object they are carrying. They could be highlighted based on battery or robot status. The prime value is the time to return to its base after completing its task.
- **Trucks** are entities that connect: (1) retailers-retailers; (2) retailers-warehouses, and (3) warehouse-warehouse, and hence consist of their location (geo) of start and end point. Trucks also have a sustainability index and activity, measured in hours.
- **Notes and stakeholders** card is shared across all the three levels and also have an ability to be highlighted to display the notes and stakeholder of choice on the home screen. Notes consist of an ID (string), the text field (string), the data of addition (string), author ID (string) and the highlight tag (bool) and type (string). Stakeholder consists of the ID (string), name (string), email (string), type (string), phone (num). The author ID of the notes is linked to the stakeholder ID to identify where the note is coming from.

C. Data Connections

All the entities are connected to each other and share data as per the linked data structure. Stakeholders and Notes are present in all the three levels of the data visualizations, but their ids are linked to their respective levels (Figure 2). For example, a stakeholder responsible for Retailer 1 has its ID linked to the ID of the retailer. At the supply chain level, the trucks are linked to the warehouse and the retailers as their locations (to and from) with the time left to complete the task as the primary variable.

At the warehouse level, the position of the robots is used to define the interior map layout of the warehouse. They carry boxes that have unique ids.

At the intelligent agent level, information related to the interoperability between robots is visualized through data about interaction and memory usage of the agents.

D. Level 1: Supply Chain level

The purpose of the Supply Chain level is to visualize data available outside the warehouse scope and how the objects in the warehouse interact with the outside environment (suppliers, retailers, and warehouse). The dashboard is divided into 5 cards: (1) Capacity, (2) Truck Journey, (3) Profitability vs. Risk Curve, (4) Notes, and (5) Stakeholders.

- **Capacity:** The capacity card details the available space in the current / adjoining warehouses along with the space available at the retailers. The data is represented by a dial visualization to give stronger emphasis to the color and the percentage value of availability. This section can be updated to check the average capacity of the warehouse or the retailer over the month, week or even year.

- **Ongoing truck journey** card details the connection journey between (1) warehouse-retailer; (2) retailer-retailer; (3) warehouse-warehouse; and depicts the current state of the journey as a progress bar. Since there is a lot more data available for the truck (Figure 3), it could be displayed on clicking the View more button next to every truck progress bar.

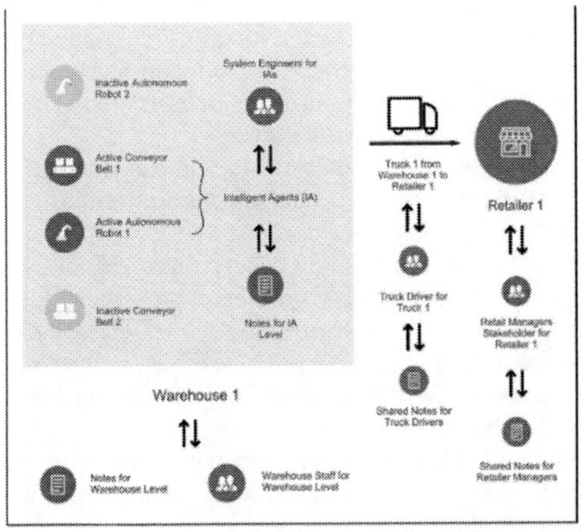

Figure 2. An overview of Warehouse 1 with different kinds of active robots (Autonomous Robot 1 and Conveyor Belt 1) being managed by system engineers.

- **Profitability vs. risk curve** is an X-Y plot with Profitability/Risk on the Y-axis and the time on the X-axis. The curve could be updated to accommodate daily, weekly monthly and yearly values. This curve represents the profits (in %) and related risk generated from the warehouse while dealing with different retailers.
- **Notes and stakeholders.** Stakeholders for the supply chain level are the truck drivers, warehouse managers, and retail managers and they have the option to add and share notes between each other.

E. Level 2: Warehouse level

The purpose of the Warehouse level is to visualize the movement and exchange of data inside the warehouse primarily by the robots. The dashboard is divided into (1) Real-time map of the warehouse, (2) Stacked-Performance Chart, (3) Robots, (4) Notes, and (5) Stakeholders.

- **Real-time map** of warehouse depicts the top view of the warehouse with robots being placed by the waypoints [7], X (Line - <num>) - Y (Y - <num>) coordinates as circles with the size of the circle representative of the battery of the robots and the intensity of the color signifying the activity state of the robot. To view more information on the robot like the danger zone, destination and the ID of the object being carried, any robot can be clicked to display that information (Figure 4).

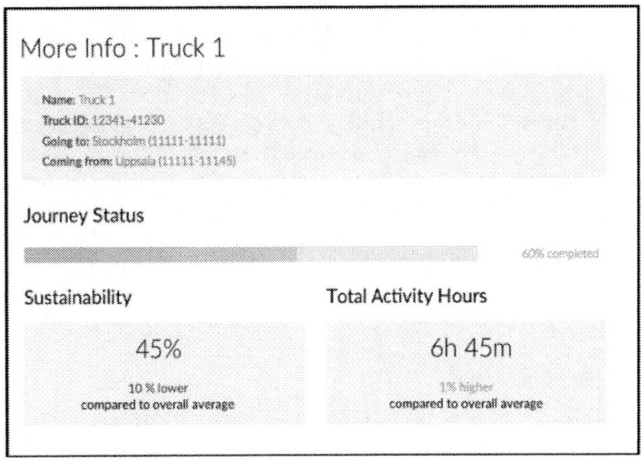

Figure 3. The modal with secondary information about the truck including the total activity hours and the Sustainability Index.

- **Stacked performance chart** gives the stakeholders an ability to select the robots from all the active robots in the warehouse and check their performance index varying from 0 - 100. The different types of robots are represented by different colors. This chart could be updated based on daily, weekly, monthly and yearly performance for further analysis (Figure 5).
- **Battery status of robots** card signifies the battery status of the robots as a primary value, which is also represented in a map state (Figure 4). Clicking on the 'view all' button reveals more information on the robot-like time left to return, the performance percent of that robot and how it is performing compared to the overall warehouse average.
- **Notes and stakeholders.** Stakeholders for the warehouse level are the warehouse managers and robot operators and they have the ability to share notes with everyone or one another.

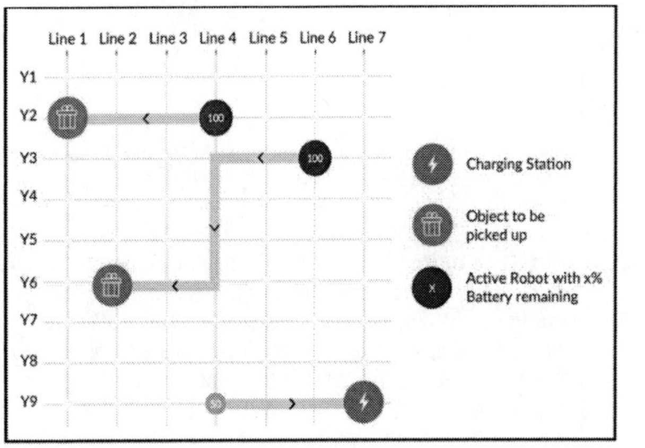

Figure 4. An overhead map of Warehouse

F. Level 3: Intelligent Agent level

The purpose of the intelligent agent level is to visualize intelligence and interoperability related concerns of the robots. The dashboard is divided into (1) Interoperability Curve, (2) Activity Monitor, (3) Notes, and (4) Stakeholders cards.

- **Robot interoperability curve** is an updatable chord diagram that has all the axis as robots in the warehouse represented by different colors. This interdependence allows the stakeholders to monitor robots when they perform a particular task. This curve can be updated on a daily, weekly monthly and yearly basis (Figure 6).

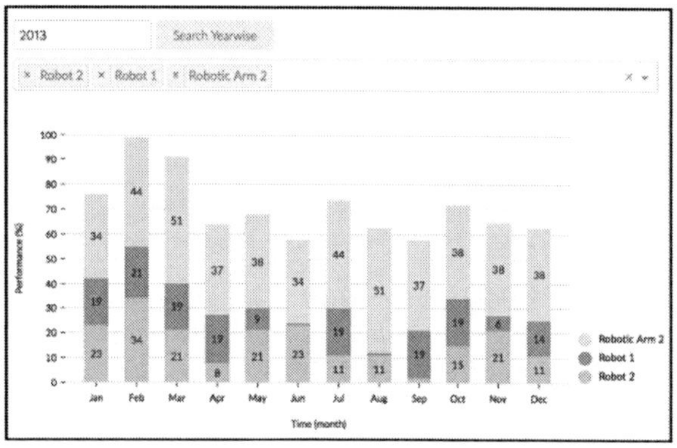

Figure 5. Stacking different robots in the warehouse with each other to compare the performance of their combination for the year 2013.

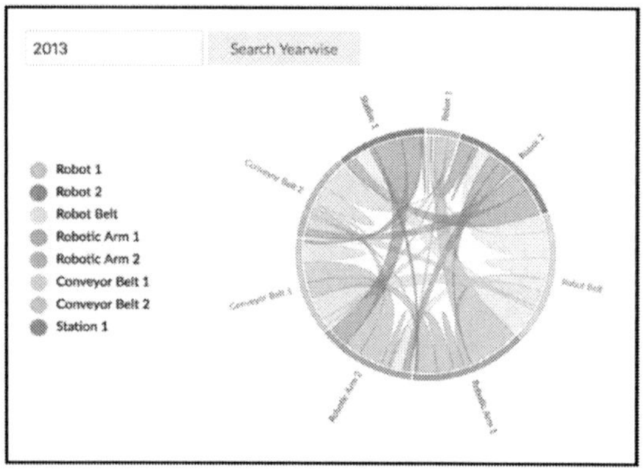

Figure 6. A chord diagram was used to visualize the interoperability between all the available robots present in Warehouse 1 for the year of 2013.

- **Activity monitor** details the connection points of the robots, with the prime value as the percentage of the job completed. When a user clicks the 'view all' button, more information about the performance of the robot is revealed such as, the start and end point, the objects being transported and the overall active hours. This information is deeply connected to the information from the real-time map and the battery status in the warehouse levels.
- **Notes and stakeholders**, the main stakeholders of this level are the system engineers, robot maintainers, and the warehouse managers. They have an ability to add and share notes between each other.

IV. USER STUDY

The final interview was conducted with 5 stakeholders who took part in the development of the automated warehouse project. These interviewees come from different domains including design, software development, systems engineering and robotics. The interview was conducted in a one-to-one semi-structured way. The length of every interview varied between 20 to 30 minutes with both the interviewer and interviewee discussing the use case of the dashboard relevant to their domain of knowledge. The interview was conducted in an uninterrupted open environment and the response was handwritten. The general structure of the interview included:

1) Introduction of the interviewer and the interviewee, the roles in the project and discussion about the first feedback iteration.

2) Primary discussion about SCOTT project and the prior experience with the dashboard and the data architecture.

3) A think-aloud session of using the dashboard exploring different levels and asking questions before switching levels with additional efforts to find the answers within the dashboard.

4) Questions the interviewee had with respect to the cards most relevant to the interviewees. What works for them and what does not?

5) Optional hands-on exercise: If any visualization is not clear, is there a better way to represent a data?

V. RESULTS

Based on the interview feedback, it was evident that defining KPI, in the beginning, proved out to be a crucial step to make the dashboard unified. During the hands-on exercise, four out of five stakeholders preferred using the chord interoperability diagram due to prior experience with a similar visualization while one stakeholder suggested using a tree-map visualization to represent the same data. Three stakeholders suggested giving preference to data susceptible to daily changes instead of data closer to the three KPI under consideration that does not update frequently. Four out of five stakeholders felt using size to represent the amount of battery left, on the warehouse map was confusing as compared to using colors to depict the same data. All the stakeholders preferred fetching only highlighted data on the dashboard instead of the entire data set on the first load because of the decrease in page load speed. Two stakeholders suggested using stakeholder hierarchy to customize the available data could be used to further simplify the visualization. For our use case, the warehouse managers could have access to all three levels of the dashboard while the systems engineers could only access the intelligent agent level.

VI. Discussion

A. Using three KPI as a starting point

Before the implementation of the visualization, two earlier studies [3][7] were conducted to identify KPI, stakeholders and the data model as the basis of deciding what kind of data would be presented on the dashboard, for whom and by what data which turned out to be extremely helpful to make both, data streams and, the dashboard uniform. At this stage, a minimal set of required data was selected, which was to be used only for monitoring purposes.

B. Expert opinion as an evaluation technique

Despite the exploratory nature of this study, we tried to validate the dashboard using a structured approach. Using expert opinion at the preliminary stage of the research proved out to be a fast and efficient way to build the prototype and identify the direction of future development. So, if these expert evaluations are not performed prior to formative evaluations, the formative evaluations will typically take longer and require more users, and yet reveal many of the same usability problems that could generally have been discovered by less expensive heuristic evaluations [14]. Thus, expert evaluations can reduce the cost of formative studies.

C. Cognitive bias in visualizations used

In terms of the visualizations used, there was a strong bias towards the visualizations used by the stakeholders for a prior similar data set, which greatly reduced the learning curve for the dashboard. The bias was expressed in the final feedback from the stakeholders when the data visualizations were fully functional. This feedback was not expressed in the earlier feedback session. This is a classic case of cognitive bias, which is observed when similar design patterns (or, in our case, data visualizations) are used frequently [15].

VII. Conclusion And Future Work

Future work will be to extend the above dashboard to incorporate real-time data streams from a working warehouse. We will continue to work on the dashboard and customize the dashboard to further to improve the user experience in the light of the feedback we received after the interviews. Furthermore, we plan to employ user-centered methodologies in the form of research tools like eye-tracking and heat-maps, to capture participant behaviour while performing certain tasks within the dashboard to draw clear conclusions.

Acknowledgment

The authors gratefully acknowledge the support from Ericsson Research, Cognitive Automation Lab. The research leading to these results has received funding from the "SCOTT -Secure Connected Trustable Things." SCOTT (www.scottproject.eu) has received funding from the Electronic Component Systems for European Leadership Joint Undertaking under grant agreement No. 737422. This Joint Undertaking receives support from the European Union's Horizon 2020 research and innovation program and Austria, Spain, Finland, Ireland, Sweden, Germany, Poland, Portugal, Netherlands, Belgium, and Norway.

References

[1] R. Rajkumar, I. Lee, L. Sha and J. Stankovic, "Cyber-Physical systems: the next computing revolution," *In Proceedings of the 47th Design Automation Conference (DAC '10)*. ACM, New York, NY, USA, pp. 731-736, 2010.

[2] E. A. Lee, "Cyber Physical Systems: Design Challenges," 11th IEEE International Symposium on Object and Component-Oriented Real-Time Distributed Computing (ISORC), pp. 363-369, 2008.

[3] D. Gürdür, K. Raizer, and J. El-Khoury, "Data Visualization Support for Complex Logistics Operations and Cyber-Physical Systems," *Proceedings of the 13th International Joint Conference on Computer Vision, Imaging and Computer Graphics Theory and Applications*, 2018.

[4] M. J. Clayton, "Delphi: a technique to harness expert opinion for critical decision-making tasks in education," *Educational Psychology*, vol. 17, no. 4, pp. 373–386, 1997.

[5] S. E. Hove and B. Anda, "Experiences from conducting semi-structured interviews in empirical software engineering research," *11th IEEE International Software Metrics Symposium (METRICS'05)*. IEEE, pp. 10-pp, 2005.

[6] R. Longhurst. Semi-structured interviews and focus groups. *Key methods in geography*, 117-132, 2003

[7] D. Gürdür, "Knowledge Representation of Cyber-physical Systems for Monitoring Purpose." *51st CIRP Conference on Manufacturing Systems (CIRP CMS 2018)*. Elsevier, 2018.

[8] G. Kahl, S. Warwas, P. Liedtke, L. Spassova and B. Brandherm, "Management dashboard in a retail scenario," in *Workshop on Location Awareness in Dual and Mixed Reality. International Conference on Intelligent User Interfaces*. IUI-11, pp. 22-25.

[9] J. E Laird and P. Rosenbloom, The evolution of the Soar cognitive architecture. *Mind matters: A tribute to Allen Newell*, 1996, pp. 1-50.

[10] G. Taylor, R. M. Jones, M. Goldstein, R. Frederiksen and R. E. Wray III, "VISTA: A generic toolkit for visualizing agent behaviour," *Ann Arbor, 1001*, 2002.

[11] B. Frost, "Designing systems—atomic design by brad frost," *Consultado em 16*, 2015.

[12] G. Ellis and D. Alan, "A taxonomy of clutter reduction for information visualization," *IEEE transactions on visualization and computer graphics 13*(6), pp. 1216-1223, 2007.

[13] D. Hix, J. E. Swan, J. L. Gabbard, M. McGee, J. Durbin and T. King, "User-centered design and evaluation of a real-time battlefield visualization virtual environment," In *Virtual Reality, 1999. Proceedings*. IEEE, pp. 96-103, 1999.

[14] J. Liedtka, "Perspective: Linking design thinking with innovation outcomes through cognitive bias reduction," In *Journal of Product Innovation Management*, *32*(6), pp. 925-938, 2015.

[15] A. M. Vipul and P. Sonpatki. ReactJS by Example-Building Modern Web Applications with React. Packt Publishing Ltd, 2016

[16] N. Q. Zhu, Data visualization with D3. js cookbook. Packt Publishing Ltd, 2013.

GraphJ: A Tool for Big Data Complexity Reduction

Hani Bani-Salameh

The Hashemite University
Zarqa 13115, Jordan
Email: hani@hu.edu.jo

Abdullah Al-Shishani

The Hashemite University
Zarqa 13115, Jordan
Email: abdullah.asendarz@gmail.com

***Abstract*—Software developers, researchers, and industrial companies from all sectors such health, transportation, water treatment, etc., use and deal with big data in order to conduct their research and find better solutions that improve our way of life. Data scientists and software engineers are using generated big data to get accurate information and to extract the maximum value from the data available to them. Big data is applicable in many domains and can help solve many problems. However, analyzing such data is not easy due to its complexity that is resembled by the 6Vs of big data: volume, velocity, value, variety, variability, and veracity. Thus, big data reduction methods and tools are used in order to enhance the data and make it easier to analyze. This paper presents a big data complexity reduction tool called GraphJ. The proposed tool converts a rational database into a graph database, which makes unlocking knowledge patterns much easier than dealing with ordinary rational databases. A case study has been conducted to assess the usefulness and effectiveness of the proposed tool.**

Keywords*–*Big data; Reduction; Complexity; Graph; Relational database; Neo4J; GraphJ.

I. INTRODUCTION

The term of big data was originated in 1997 and was introduced by two NASA researchers, Michael Cox and David Ellsworth [1]. So far, there is no formal definition for big data, although it is referred to as complex data that are characterized by the well-known Vs properties: huge volume, high value, much variety, low veracity, and big variability that are collected from multiple data streams [2]. The world's data volume keeps growing because the data is continuously produced using numerous data streams *(e.g., mobile devices, cameras, microphones, wireless sensor networks, etc.)* [3]. Hence, such growth in data makes traditional data processing applications useless and requires huge efforts for analysis and processing [4].

Researchers and data scientists working with big data face many challenges, such as: *capturing data, data storage, data analysis, search, sharing, transfer, visualization, querying, updating and information privacy* [5]-[6]. Moreover, big data inherits the *curse of dimensionality*, meaning that the data has a massive set of dimensions, which also makes analysis and processing harder [7][8]. One of the ways to overcome such issues is big data reduction. The term *'reduce'* can relate to either the complexity or the volume of the data. By reducing the complexity and/or the volume of the data, it becomes more manageable, hence easier to analyze. Big data reduction methods can be categorized into five groups, as follows:

- **Network Theory**: or graph theory is one of the significant techniques that are used in reducing high-dimensional unstructured big data into low-dimensional structured data [9]. Trovati et al. [10] proposed a network theory-based approach to extract the topological and dynamical network properties from big data.
- **Dimension reduction**: the dimensions of the data are the attributes of that data *(i.e., id and name of a student, color and speed of a car, etc.)*. The dimensionality can be reduced by either features' selection or features' extraction. Feature selection is done by only considering the important dimensions of that data, as all the dimensions will not be needed. Feature extraction is done by merging multiple sets of dimensions to derive new ones [11]-[12].
- **Deduplication**: the data collected may contain redundancies. Redundancy is not necessarily a duplicate row in the database. Redundancy in the data can be the order of bits or block of memory that is exactly identical to another one. In such case, the original one is kept, and the copy is replaced with a pointer to the original in order to reduce the volume in use [13]-[14].
- **Graph theory**: to reduce the complexity of the data, the topological and dynamical network properties are extracted. To construct topological networks, relationships between data points are established [15]-[16].
- **Compression** [9] such methods are good to handle data reduction in terms of size by maintaining the whole data streams. Compression-based methods involve complex computations that affect the reduction process efficiency and add compression overhead cost. Many big data compression techniques are proposed by academics and researchers, including spatiotemporal, Anamorphic Stretch Transform (AST), parallel compression, sketching, and adaptive compression.

Research showed that these methods cannot be used single-handedly by considering all the Vs properties of big data [15], which motivates the need for more reliable data reduction approaches that combine multiple methods together.

Motivated by knowledge graphs [17]-[18], this paper presents a tool and an approach to reduce big data complexity using graphs. In graphs, data is presented using nodes and edges instead of using an ordinary relational database (see Figure 1), where each row is presented by a node (an object), and relationships between the entities are replaced with edges between the nodes. Presenting the database using a graph database makes the act of unlocking knowledge patterns easier

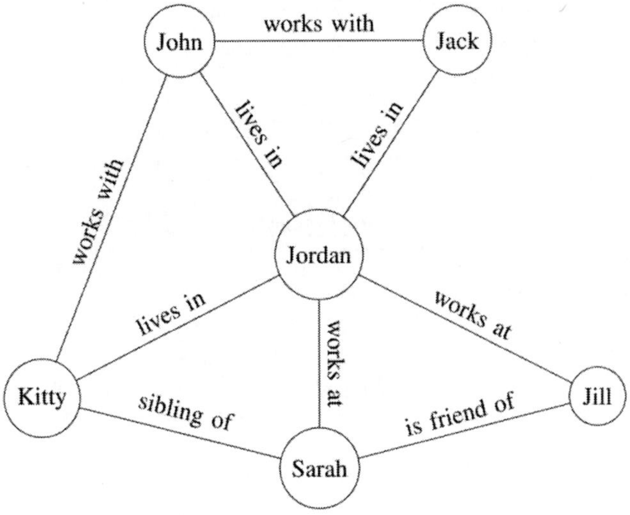

Figure 1. A sample of graph database.

[15], and is most useful when one must deal with highly interconnected data [19].

GraphJ uses MySQL database [20] to convert its schema and data into Neo4J graph database [21]. The reason for choosing MySQL because it is well known and widely used. The reason for choosing Neo4J is because of its high performance [22]-[23]. GraphJ is built using Java, because of its suitability and connectivity support for Neo4J.

The rest of this paper is organized as follows: Section II describes related work; Section III describes the tool and used approach; Section IV presents an experimental evaluation; Section V presents the conclusion.

II. Related Work

There are a lot of tools and approaches for big data reduction. Some of these methods are based on *Network Theory* [10], *Compression* [24]-[25] and others based on *Dimension Reduction* [11][12][26].

The topological properties of the networks have been used to model big datasets and study their structure that faced challenges due to the datasets complexity and dependencies between their parts. Defining the models based on such data properties makes it hard to understand the data and to produce useful information due to their complexity and the data inconsistencies. Trovati [10] introduced a big data analytics tool which allows to extract useful data and to obtain in-depth intelligence from such different big datasets.

Jalali and Asghari [24] introduce a lossy image compression that reshapes the image. It depends on the idea that if the image is sampled in a way that is the same in all cases and at all times, then the sharp features have a higher sampling density than the rough ones. This method is claimed to be applicable for big data compression.

Yang et al. [27] present a solution that makes it possible for the compression method to compress the data efficiently. The solution is based on applying the clustering method to the datasets (input data). It divides the data into several different clusters(groups), and then compress the data according to the assigned clustering information.

Dynamic Quantum Clustering (DQC) is a method that works with big and multi-dimensional data. Weinstein et al. [11] conduct studies that show how DQC works for big real-world datasets that come from five different domains, namely "x-ray nano-chemistry, condensed matter, biology, seismology, and finance". These studies show how DQC help at extracting meaningful data that contain important information. They claimed that this method establishes important results that show how complex datasets contain various different structures that might be missed by the other clustering techniques.

To our knowledge, there are currently no tools or approaches to reducing big data complexity using a graph database or knowledge graphs.

TABLE I. GraphJ Environment Variables.

Key	Data Type	Default Value
MYSQL_HOST	String	localhost
MYSQL_PORT	Integer	3306
MYSQL_USER	String	root
MYSQL_PASS	String	root
MYSQL_DB	String	null
QUERY_LIMIT	Integer	1000

III. GraphJ Tool

GraphJ is a standalone GUI based application written in JavaFX [28] and based on Spring Framework [29] for resource management. It is built to convert a MySQL database [20] into a Neo4J graph database [21]. To convert the database, GraphJ performs the following activities (see Figure 2):

1) **MySQL host**
GraphJ requires a live MySQL host to read the database schema from. There is no need to specify a database in that host because GraphJ will inspect all the databases. The connection is established to the host using MySQL Java database connectivity (JDBC) driver [30]. JDBC may not work on remote hosts due to remote direct access regulations, as most of the databases do not allow direct access to the database.
The connection is made using an interface called *DBConnection*. DBConnection contains abstract methods that allows to extract(*host, port, username, password, and database*). The *database* is used only to define the default database for the connection. To set all the required data, GraphJ reads these properties from the environment variables (see Table I).
2) **Inspect the schema**
GraphJ uses a module called *SchemaInspector*, which provides all the details about a schema under inspection. *SchemaInspector* requires an object of *DBConnection* in order to decide which *host, port, username, and password* that it will be dealing with. However, it does not require a *database* from the *DBConnection* object. It inspects all the databases on that host, as database selection is done later.

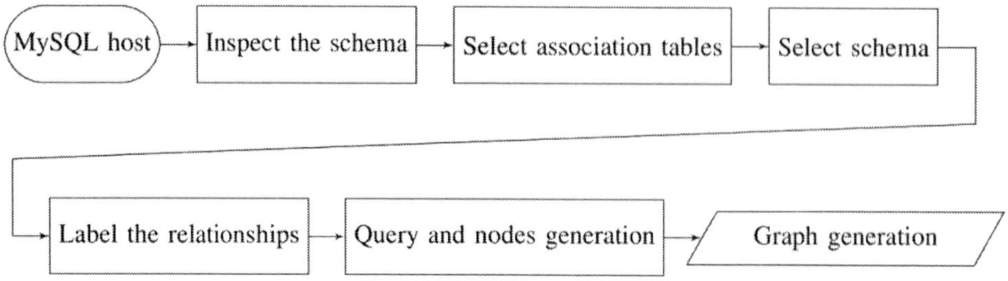

Figure 2. GraphJ flow chart.

SchemaCrawler[31] is used to read the structure of all databases on the provided host. SchemaCrawler is used, although schema can be inspected using *java.sql.DatabaseMetaData*, because it gives a full description of each table, name, columns, primary keys, foreign keys.

3) **Select association tables**
Association or join tables are tables that represent *many to many* relationships between two tables, by using the primary key of each table as foreign keys in an association table. Such tables should be referenced by the user, as they can not be identified programmatically. These tables should be referenced because they will be treated in a different way than *one to one* or *one to many* relationships, since association tables should be omitted and replaced with the original tables.

4) **Select schema**
A single schema should be selected with association tables referenced.

5) **Label the relationships**
Each relationship, including *many to many*, between the tables should be labeled in order to name the relationships between the nodes of the graph.

6) **Query and nodes generation**
GraphJ uses a module called *MySqlConnector* which requires a *DBConnection* in order to establish a connection and execute queries. The queries are executed using *java.sql.Statement*. The reason behind using it instead of *Hibernate* [32] is because HQL Queries suffer from performance degradation (because it should convert HQL to SQL [33], although the performance degradation is trivial, it becomes more tangible when executing queries repeatedly). However, even with SQL, the performance degrades if the database has massive records. To overcome this issue, the queries retrieve limited results. The limitation is read from an environment variable with the key *QUERY_LIMIT*. Inside *MySqlConnector* there are 3 main queries:

- SELECT * FROM table
  table is the table under processing.

  Select all the rows from that table, in order to create a node for each row. After the query is executed, all the attributes are inserted into the node being created. These attributes can be mapped because it is possible to know each column in each table with the help of *SchemaInspector*, each column name is the key. Attributes with a value of *null* are ignored.

- SELECT * FROM r_table WHERE f_k=o_pk
  r_table is the foreign key table.
  f_k is the foreign key in *r_table*.
  o_pk is the primary key in the table that has a relationship with *r_table*.

  Select all the rows from that table that match the foreign in the original table.

- SELECT * FROM j_table INNER JOIN r_table on r_pk=r_fk WHERE o_fk = o_pk
  j_table is the association table
  r_table is the foreign key table.
  r_pk is the primary key in the original table under processing.
  r_fk is the foreign key in *r_table*.
  o_fk is the foreign key reference to the original table under processing.
  o_pk is the primary key in the table that has a relationship with *r_table*.

  Select all the rows from that table that match the foreign in the original table.

Queries are generated based on the selected schema and the relationships between the tables.

7) **Graph generation**
Once the nodes with their relationships are created, the last step is to flush these nodes into the Neo4J database. GraphJ tries to connect to an already instantiated Neo4J database. It read the database path from an environment variable with key *NEO4J_DB*. This database's host should be stopped in order to establish a connection, as it cannot establish two connections at the same time.

IV. EXPERIMENTAL EVALUATION

In this section, experimental evaluation details, goals, and results of GraphJ are presented.

TABLE II. SUBJECT DATABASES.

Database	# tables	# all relationships	# M2M relationships	# records
World X	3	2	0	5411
Sakila	16	22	2	47271
Employees	6	6	2	3911245

TABLE III. AVERAGE TOTAL EXECUTION TIMES.

Database	Query Limit					
	500	1000	1500	2000	2500	3000
World X	16 s	26 s	33 s	40 s	50 s	60 s
Sakila	1.5 m	4 m	5.9 m	7.8 m	9.8 m	11.8 m
Employees	17 s	49 s	1.7 m	3.1 m	4.5 m	6.6 m

A. Goals

The goal was to evaluate the performance of GraphJ. Hence, and to cover all the possible cases, GraphJ has been run on two different databases, with different run configurations. In the end, the total execution time of each one of the run configurations has been compared.

B. Subject Databases

For the evaluation, MySQL sample databases [34] were used. Those databases are well known and widely used for testing MySQL queries. Three of the databases were used(see Table II):

- **World X** [35]: Provided by Oracle [36], it has a set of tables containing information on the countries and cities of the world.
- **Sakila** [37]: Provided by Oracle [36], it is designed to represent a DVD rental store. This database borrows film and actor names from the Dell sample database [38].
- **Employees** [39]: Originally developed by Patrick Crews and Giuseppe Maxia and provides a large set of data that consists of 4 million records.

C. Configuration

GraphJ ran on 64-bit Linux machine with Intel Core i5-4200M and 8 GBs of memory. The MySQL and Neo4J databases were located on *localhost* on ports 3306 and 7474. The performance can be affected by the nature of the database and the query limitations, for that, the study tried to simulate real-life cases.

D. Results

The node generation and relationship mapping are done correctly. However, the performance is questionable, thus, GraphJ ran on the three databases with query limited from 500 to 3000 increasing by 500 each time. After running the tool on the three databases (10 times for each query limitation value). The results showed that the performance is significantly affected by the number of tables and relationships, however, the number of rows does not have much effect. The average total execution times are shown in Table III.

V. CONCLUSION

This paper presents a big data complexity reduction (called GraphJ). GraphJ reads a MySQL database and maps its records to nodes in order to insert them into a Neo4J database. The tool converts a relational database into a graph database, which reduces the complexity, as graph databases facilitate the act of unlocking knowledge patterns [40].

Conversion is done by inspecting the schema of a provided relational database, including table names, column names, and column types. Then the relationships between existing tables are inspected, and the user is asked to label these relationships. After that, the queries are generated using the schema data inspected earlier. Finally, the queries are executed to generate nodes in order to be inserted into the graph database using the retrieved data. The relationships between these nodes are created based on the names the user provided. This results in a set of nodes connected together. These nodes are then inserted into a provided graph database.

To assess the effectiveness of the proposed tool, a case study was conducted. Three MySQL sample databases (World X, Sakila and Employees) were used. GraphJ ran with query limitation starting with 500 records and increasing by 500 each time until reaching 3000 records. Each relational database ran 10 times for each query limitation value. The tool was able to convert all databases into graph databases correctly. However, the results showed that the performance is significantly affected by the number of tables and relationships in the relational database.

Following are various opportunities in order to improve the proposed tool:

- Experiment: larger experiments can be performed on the proposed tool to further assess and evaluate its effectiveness.
- Database support: there are a lot of databases available and are widely used. However, the current implementation of GraphJ only supports MySQL and Neo4j. The tool can be extended to support more database implementations.

GraphJ is built using JavaFX with Spring Framework. The tool with the source code is available on GitHub repository: https://github.com/AbdullahAsendar/GraphJ.

References

[1] B. Logica and R. Magdalena, "Using big data in the academic environment," Procedia Economics and Finance, vol. 33, 2015, pp. 277–286.

[2] G. W. X. Wu, X. Zhu and W. Ding, "Data mining with big data," IEEE Trans. on Knowl. and Data Eng., vol. 26, no. 1, Jan. 2014, pp. 97–107. [Online]. Available: http://dx.doi.org/10.1109/TKDE.2013.109

[3] T. Segaran and J. Hammerbacher, Beautiful data: the stories behind elegant data solutions. " O'Reilly Media, Inc.", 2009.

[4] D. Che, M. Safran, and Z. Peng, "From big data to big data mining: challenges, issues, and opportunities," in International Conference on Database Systems for Advanced Applications. Springer, 2013, pp. 1–15.

[5] A. A. Tole et al., "Big data challenges," Database Systems Journal, vol. 4, no. 3, 2013, pp. 31–40.

[6] T. Rabl, S. Gómez-Villamor, M. Sadoghi, V. Muntés-Mulero, H.-A. Jacobsen, and S. Mankovskii, "Solving big data challenges for enterprise application performance management," Proc. VLDB Endow., vol. 5, no. 12, Aug. 2012, pp. 1724–1735. [Online]. Available: http://dx.doi.org/10.14778/2367502.2367512

[7] Y. Zhai, Y.-S. Ong, and I. W. Tsang, "The emerging" big dimensionality"," IEEE Computational Intelligence Magazine, vol. 9, no. 3, 2014, pp. 14–26.

[8] J. Fan, F. Han, and H. Liu, "Challenges of big data analysis," National science review, vol. 1, no. 2, 2014, pp. 293–314.

[9] M. H. U. Rehman, C. S. Liew, A. Abbas, P. P. Jayaraman, T. Y. Wah, and S. U. Khan, "Big data reduction methods: A survey," Data Science and Engineering, vol. 1, no. 4, 2016, pp. 265–284.

[10] M. Trovati, "Reduced topologically real-world networks: a big-data approach," International Journal of Distributed Systems and Technologies (IJDST), vol. 6, no. 2, 2015, pp. 13–27.

[11] M. Weinstein, F. Meirer, A. Hume, P. Sciau, G. Shaked, R. Hofstetter, E. Persi, A. Mehta, and D. Horn, "Analyzing big data with dynamic quantum clustering," arXiv preprint arXiv:1310.2700, 2013.

[12] D. Feldman, M. Schmidt, and C. Sohler, "Turning big data into tiny data: Constant-size coresets for k-means, pca and projective clustering," in Proceedings of the twenty-fourth annual ACM-SIAM symposium on Discrete algorithms. SIAM, 2013, pp. 1434–1453.

[13] Y. Fu, H. Jiang, and N. Xiao, "A scalable inline cluster deduplication framework for big data protection," in Proceedings of the 13th international middleware conference. Springer-Verlag New York, Inc., 2012, pp. 354–373.

[14] W. Xia, H. Jiang, D. Feng, and Y. Hua, "Silo: A similarity-locality based near-exact deduplication scheme with low ram overhead and high throughput," in USENIX annual technical conference, 2011, pp. 26–30.

[15] M. Chen, S. Mao, and Y. Liu, "Big data: A survey," Mobile Networks and Applications, vol. 19, no. 2, 2014, pp. 171–209.

[16] A. C. Wilkerson, H. Chintakunta, and H. Krim, "Computing persistent features in big data: A distributed dimension reduction approach," in ICASSP, 2014, pp. 11–15.

[17] A. Singhal, "Introducing the knowledge graph: things, not strings," Official google blog, 2012.

[18] O. Corby and C. F. Zucker, "The kgram abstract machine for knowledge graph querying," in Web Intelligence and Intelligent Agent Technology (WI-IAT), 2010 IEEE/WIC/ACM International Conference on, vol. 1. IEEE, 2010, pp. 338–341.

[19] J. Hurwitz, A. Nugent, F. Halper, and M. Kaufman, Big Data For Dummies, 1st ed. For Dummies, 2013.

[20] A. MySQL, "Mysql," 2001.

[21] N. Developers, "Neo4j," Graph NoSQL Database [online], 2012.

[22] C. Vicknair, M. Macias, Z. Zhao, X. Nan, Y. Chen, and D. Wilkins, "A comparison of a graph database and a relational database: a data provenance perspective," in Proceedings of the 48th annual Southeast regional conference. ACM, 2010, p. 42.

[23] H. Huang and Z. Dong, "Research on architecture and query performance based on distributed graph database neo4j," in Consumer Electronics, Communications and Networks (CECNet), 2013 3rd International Conference on. IEEE, 2013, pp. 533–536.

[24] B. Jalali and M. H. Asghari, "The anamorphic stretch transform: Putting the squeeze on big data," Optics and Photonics News, vol. 25, no. 2, 2014, pp. 24–31.

[25] K. Ackermann and S. D. Angus, "A resource efficient big data analysis method for the social sciences: the case of global ip activity," Procedia Computer Science, vol. 29, 2014, pp. 2360–2369.

[26] C.-J. Hsieh, M. A. Sustik, I. S. Dhillon, P. K. Ravikumar, and R. Poldrack, "Big & quic: Sparse inverse covariance estimation for a million variables," in Advances in neural information processing systems, 2013, pp. 3165–3173.

[27] C. Yang, X. Zhang, C. Zhong, C. Liu, J. Pei, K. Ramamohanarao, and J. Chen, "A spatiotemporal compression based approach for efficient big data processing on cloud," Journal of Computer and System Sciences, vol. 80, no. 8, 2014, pp. 1563–1583.

[28] J. Clarke, J. Connors, and E. J. Bruno, JavaFX: developing rich Internet applications. Pearson Education, 2009.

[29] R. Johnson, J. Hoeller, A. Arendsen, and R. Thomas, Professional Java development with the Spring framework. John Wiley & Sons, 2009.

[30] G. Hamilton, R. Cattell, M. Fisher et al., JDBC Database Access with Java. Addison Wesley, 1997, vol. 7.

[31] D. O'Neill, "Id3. org," Sualeh Fatehi," SchemaCrawler". SourceForge.[Online]. Available: http://www. its. bldrdoc. gov/fs-1037/fs-1037c. htm (visited March.

[32] C. Bauer and G. King, Java Persistance with Hibernate. Dreamtech Press, 2006.

[33] ——, Hibernate in Action. Greenwich, CT: Manning, 2005. [Online]. Available: http://www.amazon.com/Hibernate-Action-In-Christian-Bauer/dp/193239415X

[34] "MySQL sample databases," https://dev.mysql.com/doc/index-other.html, last accessed: February 9, 2019.

[35] "World X sample database," https://dev.mysql.com/doc/world-setup/en/, last accessed: February 9, 2019.

[36] K. Loney, Oracle Database 10g The Complete Reference, ser. Oracle Press. McGraw-Hill Education, 2004. [Online]. Available: https://books.google.jo/books?id=qMk3xkkIv0QC

[37] "Sakila sample database," https://dev.mysql.com/doc/sakila/en/, last accessed: February 9, 2019.

[38] "Dell dvd store database," https://linux.dell.com/dvdstore/, last accessed: February 9, 2019.

[39] "Employees sample database," https://dev.mysql.com/doc/employee/en/, last accessed: February 9, 2019.

[40] L. Bellomarini, G. Gottlob, A. Pieris, and E. Sallinger, "Swift logic for big data and knowledge graphs," in Proceedings of the Twenty-Sixth International Joint Conference on Artificial Intelligence, IJCAI-17, 2017, pp. 2–10. [Online]. Available: https://doi.org/10.24963/ijcai.2017/1

Real-Time Big Data Analytics for Traffic Monitoring and Management for Pedestrian and Cyclist Safety

Mohammad Pourhomayoun, Haiyan Wang, Mohammad Vahedi, Mehran Mazari
Computer Science Department
California State University Los Angeles
Email: mpourho@calstatela.edu, hwang2@calstatela.edu, mvahedi@calstatela.edu, mmazari2@calstatela.edu

Hunter Owens
Data Science Federation
City of Los Angeles
Los Angeles, USA
Email: hunter.owens@lacity.org

Janna Smith
Department of Transportation
City of Los Angeles, Los Angeles, USA
Email: janna.smith@lacity.org

William Chernicoff
Toyota Mobility Foundation
Washington DC, USA
Email: william.chernicoff@toyota.com

Abstract— **In this study, we design and develop an end-to-end system based on data analytics and deep learning methods to monitor, count, and manage traffic, particularly, pedestrians and bicyclists in real-time. The main objective of this research is to improve the safety of pedestrians and bicyclists, by applying self-sensed and intelligent systems to control and monitor the flow of pedestrians/bicyclists particularly at intersections. This paper proposes an effective end-to-end system for traffic vision, detection, and counting on real-time traffic videos. The developed system is evaluated on 12 hours of real video streams captured from actual traffic cameras in the city of Los Angeles. According to the results, the developed system can count the pedestrians with less than 2% error.**

Keywords - Machine Learning; Deep Learning; Computer Vision; Object Detection.

I. INTRODUCTION

By 2050, 66% of the world's population is projected to be urban [1][2]. As urban populations rise, it is essential for city designers and planners to focus more on designing smart cities and addressing the main challenges, such as traffic issues, and the impacts of increased vehicle use. According to the U.S. Department of Transportation (USDOT), the number of traffic fatalities has increased by nearly 6% in 2016 [3]. The number of traffic fatalities only in the state of California was 3,623 in 2016, which is more than 9.2 deaths per 100,000 population.

Understanding the movement of people, bicycles, and their interaction with vehicles is critical to avoid traffic accidents and improve safety. We know that the most vulnerable components of the traffic collisions are pedestrians and bicyclists. Thus, it is essential to develop intelligent transportation systems, and human-centered traffic approaches to protect our pedestrians and cyclists and ensure that they can travel safely, efficiently, and comfortably.

With the advancement of technology, automated traffic monitoring has been gaining attraction over the past couple of years. In particular, several methods have been proposed for pedestrian detection in the past couple of years [4] – [6]. These methods have used different techniques including image/video processing, as well as machine learning techniques to detect human targets (pedestrian). Most of the previous contributions have used standard datasets including images/videos captured in ideal situations to evaluate the performance of the algorithm [5]. However, when we want to do it in practice, in real-time on video streams from traffic cameras in the scale of a large city like Los Angeles, it will be very different from lab settings, and we need to deal with challenges of Big Data Analytics.

Dollar et al. [4] and Beneson et al. [5] performed an extensive evaluation of the state of the practice. They put together the most popular pedestrian datasets and evaluated the performance of the most promising pedestrian detectors across several datasets. They have shown that despite significant progress in the past few years, the performance still has much room for improvement. Particularly, the pedestrian detection results are disappointing at low resolutions videos and for occluded pedestrians in the image [4].

The goal of this study is to design and develop an end-to-end system based on computer vision and machine learning to monitor, detect, track, count, and manage traffic, particularly, pedestrians and bicyclists. In this paper, we will evaluate our system on 12 hours of real video streams captured from actual traffic cameras in the city of Los Angeles. According to the results, the developed system can count the pedestrians with less than 2% error.

The rest of the paper is organized as follows: Section II describes the system architecture, methods, and the details of the proposed framework and components. Section III provides the evaluation results on actual data including 12 hours of real video streams captured from actual traffic cameras in the city of Los Angeles. Finally, Section IV includes the conclusion.

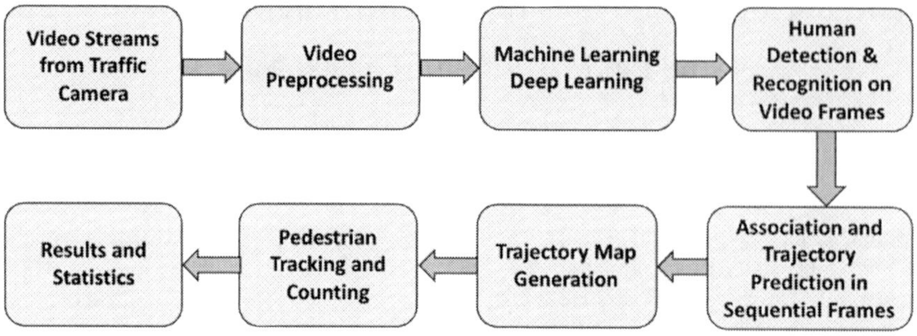

Figure 1. End-to-end system architecture.

II. System Architecture and Method

In this study, we have developed an end-to-end system including a series of image/video processing, computer vision algorithms, Machine Learning and Deep Learning, and optimal state estimator algorithms that receive video streams in real-time, and detect, recognize, track, and count pedestrians and cyclists in the video.

Figure 1 shows the high-level system architecture. The first step in the proposed traffic vision system is raw video preprocessing, which includes a series of algorithms for quality enhancement, and brightness/contrast adjustment. In the case of wide-angle lenses that may make the image convex, we can also use correction algorithms to convert the video back to natural view.

An important step in video preprocessing is background estimation and subtraction. In this concept, any moving object is considered as foreground, and any stationary object (i.e., an object with fixed location in a number of sequential frames) is considered as background. Although most of machine learning algorithms can still perform object recognition without a background removal step, but most of the time, it can improve the performance and accuracy of object recognition algorithm and also reduce the computational load of the object recognition algorithm by reducing the size of the area of interest.

In this study, we tried several effective algorithms for background estimation/subtraction including mean filter, frame differencing, running Gaussian average, and Mixture of Gaussian modeling (MOG) [6][7]. It turned out that MOG, and also mean filtering achieved the best results for background subtraction. Figure 2 shows the results of background subtraction (i.e., moving object detection) based on mean filtering. We have to note that the background continuously changes because the light direction and intensity changes. Thus, it is essential to continuously estimate and update the background to always have the best background subtraction performance.

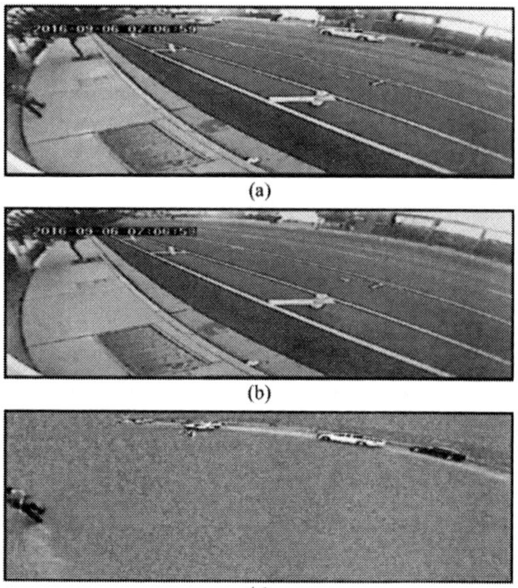

(a)

(b)

(c)

Figure 2. Background subtraction: (a) Original video frame, (b) Estimated background, (c) Moving objects after background subtraction.

After video preprocessing, the next step is to extract and select the best set of computer vision features that can be used in machine learning algorithms for object detection. Depending on the type of machine learning algorithm, this step may include feature extraction, feature selection, and/or dimensionality reduction. We have tried many different types of features and machine learning algorithms for object recognition.

Before recent advancement in deep learning, Histogram of Oriented Gradient (HOG) has been one of the most popular hand-made features for object recognition [8]. HOG features along with Support Vector Machine (SVM) classifier can form an effective method for pedestrian recognition [8]. HOG is a feature descriptor that counts occurrences of gradient orientation in localized portions of an image [8].

In this study, we have also tried various deep learning methods, particularly the Convolutional Neural Networks (ConvNet), R-CNN (Region-based Convolutional Network), and YOLO (You Only Look Once) algorithms [9]-[12]. A big advantage of ConvNet methods compared to other classic machine learning algorithms is that there is no need to generate and use hand-made features for ConvNet. The algorithm automatically learns to generate the best set of convolutional features that can best represent the image. However, ConvNet is computationally expensive and sometimes difficult to run in real-time on high-frame-rate videos. In addition, when the training dataset is not large enough, it is usually hard to train an accurate deep neural network. In this case, Transfer Learning methods that take advantage of a pre-trained neural network model on other dataset can be very helpful to expedite the training stage [14].

Figure 3-(a) shows our pedestrian detection results on an actual traffic video using HOG features and SVM classifier. Figure 3-(b) shows our results using YOLO algorithm.

(a)

(b)

Figure 3. Pedestrian detection using machine learning algorithms. (a) using HOG features and SVM classifier, (b) using YOLO.

After detecting/recognizing the object of interest (e.g., a pedestrian or bicyclist) in several sequential frames, we use *Optimal State Estimator* to estimate the *Trajectory* of each target object. Since several objects may exist in each frame at a time (e.g., several pedestrians walking together in same direction or different directions), it is essential to estimate the trajectory of each object individually.

We use Kalman Filter [13] as an optimal state estimator to predict the next location of the object and estimate the trajectory of the object over time. In this approach, in addition to the location of each bounding box, we extract and use a set of object features to represent each object uniquely. This allows us to recognize, distinguish, and track each object (i.e., each pedestrian or bicyclist) individually during the video, especially in difficult situations when several objects pass or overlap each other.

Suppose that we want to track a pedestrian. We use Kalman filter to predict the next location of each pedestrian in the next frame based on the previous locations and walking pace (extracted from previous frames). Then, after receiving the next frame, we compare our prediction with the new pedestrian detected in the next frame. The association is performed by comparing the bounding box location as well as other object features. This comparison tells us if this pedestrian was the same person in the previous frame, or it is a new one. If the predicted location and actual location match, we consider this pedestrian as previous one, and continue completing the trajectory of this pedestrian (see Figure 4). Using this approach, we can build a trajectory map including individual trajectories for all pedestrians in the video, and then track each pedestrian from the first frame he enters until the last frame when he moves out.

Figure 4. Location prediction and Trajectory estimation.

In this approach, when we detect a pedestrian whose location does not match to any of the previously predicted locations (it does not locate on any of the existing estimated trajectories), we consider that person as a new pedestrian and consequently, increment the pedestrian counter. This will allow us to track and count each pedestrian everywhere in the scene, and avoid double counting them in sequential frames.

III. RESULTS ON ACTUAL DATA

We evaluated our developed system on 12 hours of real video streams captured from actual traffic cameras in the city of Los Angeles. Figure 5 shows some of the results for pedestrian and bicyclist detection, tracking, and counting.

Table 1 shows the pedestrian counting results on the video streams captured from an actual traffic camera in the city of Los Angeles for 12 hours (a view of the camera is shown in Figure 5-b). The first column of Table 1 shows the hour number; the second column shows the number of pedestrians counted automatically by the developed system; the third column shows the actual number of pedestrians counted by a human expert as the ground truth; and the last column is the hourly percent error. The last row in Table 1 shows the Overall Percent Error of 1.7% for counting over 12 hours. We used the following equation to calculate the Percent Error:

$$\text{Percent Error } = \frac{|\,A - B\,|}{B} * 100$$

where A is the number of pedestrian counted automatically by the developed system, and B is the correct number of pedestrians counted by a human expert.

(a) (b)

Figure 5. System results on real-time traffic video streams: (a) Bicyclist tracking and counting, (b) Pedestrian tracking and counting.

TABLE I. PEDESTRIAN COUNTING RESULTS FOR REAL VIDEO STREAMS CAPTURED FROM TRAFFIC CAMERAS IN LOS ANGELES FOR 12 HOURS (A VIEW OF THE CAMERA IS SHOWN IN FIGURE 5-B).

Hour No	Automated Counted by Developed System	Ground Truth Counted by Human	Hourly Error
1	89	86	3.5%
2	94	90	4.4%
3	101	107	5.6%
4	148	139	6.5%
5	120	110	9.1%
6	153	160	4.4%
7	217	210	3.3%
8	242	234	3.4%
9	222	229	3.1%
10	260	261	0.4%
11	331	324	2.2%
12	291	280	3.9%
Total	**2268**	**2230**	
Average of Hourly Errors = 4.1%			
Overall Percent Error in 12 hours = 1.7%			

IV. CONCLUSION

This paper introduced an effective end-to-end system based on computer vision and machine learning to detect, recognize, monitor, track, and count pedestrians and bicyclists in real-time. This approach particularly enables us to recognize and monitor busy intersections that are prone to traffic accidents, and allows us to control and manage traffic in those intersections to protect our pedestrians and bicyclists.

The California State University Los Angeles in partnership with the Los Angeles Department of Transportation (LADOT), the City of Los Angeles, and Toyota Mobility Foundation has developed this effective and scalable system to detect, monitor, track, and count pedestrians and bicyclists in real-time. This system is potentially scalable to the 56,000 miles of streets in Los Angeles. Despite many practical challenges, the developed system works very well with the existing regular traffic cameras and therefore, there is no need to install any special or new cameras for this purpose.

ACKNOWLEDGMENT

The authors would like to thank Toyota Mobility Foundation for supporting this research. The authors would like to thank LADOT, City of LA, and ITA Data Science Federation for valuable help and support.

REFERENCES

[1] World Urbanization Prospects, UN-Department of Economic and Social Affairs, 2018.

[2] Unicef, www.unicef.org/sowc2012/urbanmap, 2012.

[3] USDOT, https://www.nhtsa.gov/press-releases/usdot-releases-2016-fatal-traffic-crash-data, 2016.

[4] P. Dollar, C. Wojek, B. Schiele, P. Perona, "Pedestrian Detection: An Evaluation of the State of the Art," in IEEE Trans. on Pattern Analysis and Machine Intelligence, vol 34, p.p 743 – 761, 2012.

[5] R. Benenson, et al. "Ten Years of Pedestrian Detection, What Have We Learned?" ECCV, Springer, pp 613-627, 2015.

[6] N. Dalal and B. Triggs, "Histograms of oriented gradients for human detection," IEEE CVPR'05, Jun 2005.

[7] M. Piccardi, "Background subtraction techniques: a review", IEEE Int. Conf. on Systems, Man and Cybernetics, 2004.

[8] T. Bouwman, F. El Baf, B. Vachon, "Background Modeling using Mixture of Gaussians for Foreground Detection – A Survey". Recent Patents on Comp. Science, pp. 219-237, 2008.

[9] R. Girshick, "Fast R-CNN," IEEE International Conference on Computer Vision (ICCV), 2015.

[10] S. Ren, K. He, R. Girshick, J. Sun, "Faster R-CNN: Towards Real-Time Object Detection with Region Proposal Networks," IEEE Trans. Pattern Analysis & Machine Intelligence, 2017.

[11] J. Redmon, S. Divvala, R. Girshick, A. Farhadi, "You Only Look Once:Unified, Real-Time Object Detection," Computer Vision & Pattern Recog., 2016.

[12] A. Krizhevsky, I. Sutskever, G. Hinton, "ImageNet Classification with Deep Convolutional Neural Networks", NIPS 2012.

[13] P. Zarchan and H. Musoff, "Fundamentals of Kalman Filtering: A Practical Approach", ISBN 978-1-56347-455-2, 2000.

[14] H. Wang, et al., "An End-to-End Traffic Vision and Counting System Using Computer Vision and Machine Learning: The Challenges in Real-Time Processing", SIGNAL2018, 2018.

Towards Gateless Railway Services using GPS Location Based Ride Detection

Jun Nemoto

Graduate School of Science and Technology
Keio University
Yokohama, Japan
Email: nemoto@keio.jp

Motomichi Toyama

Faculty of Science and Technology
Keio University
Yokohama, Japan
Email: toyama@ics.keio.ac.jp

***Abstract*—Gateless ticket inspection is an interesting and attractive feature that can help achieve less waiting, less fare evasion, less difficulty of use for railway services for everyone, including physically handicapped people. In this paper, we study ride route detection using Global Positioning System (GPS) as a new approach for implementing gateless railway services. We assume the gateless railway service has access to the user's GPS location through an application on their smartphone or another mobile device. This position can then be compared with the GPS location of trains in order to detect the stations at which the user boarded and disembarked. Then, railway operators can charge the user for the ride. A challenge in the ride detection for fare charge in railway services is to detect the ride correctly, even if the GPS trajectory is short, e.g., in case users only ride for one station. In order to solve this challenge, we propose a ride detection solution that uses different criteria to evaluate how far the user and train were moving between two stations. In our simulation using railway line open data provided by the Ministry of Land, Infrastructure, Transport and Tourism (MLIT) in Japan, we show that our proposed method reduced false positives by 25%-100% in most cases.**

Keywords–GPS; GIS; Railway Ride Detection.

I. Introduction

Gateless ticket inspection is an interesting and attractive feature that can help achieve less waiting, less fare evasion, less difficulty of use of railway services for everyone, including physically handicapped people. For example, a barrier-free fare collection system using wireless communication technology has been proposed in [1]. It enables wheelchair users and people with strollers or big luggage to pass smoothly without using a smart card or ticket at the gate.

In this paper, we study ride detection using GPS location as a new approach for implementing gateless railway services. We assume the gateless railway service has access to the user's GPS location through an application on their smartphone, or another mobile device. This position can then be compared with the GPS location of trains in order to detect the stations at which the user boarded and disembarked. Then, railway operators can charge the user for the ride.

There has been a lot of research on transportation mode detection using GPS location [2]–[7]. These works have proposed to infer a user's mode of transportation, such as walking, car, and rail based on the velocity calculated by trajectories of GPS location, data of accelerometers, Geographic Information System (GIS) data, and so on. However, all of them do not discuss ride detection but focus on transportation mode detection. In the ride detection, we need to know not only that a user rode a train but exactly which train the user rode because, for example, two operators could run trains on the same line.

A challenge in ride detection for fare charging in railway services is to detect the ride correctly even if the GPS trajectory is short. It is not difficult to infer the transportation mode if a user's GPS trajectory is relatively long across multiple stations, as noise in the data can be averaged out, and data preceding and following a time point can be used for inference (e.g., if a user rode a train between A and B and C and D they probably also rode it between B and C). A gateless railway service needs to accurately charge all rides, even short ones so we take the harder case of short GPS trajectories into particular consideration.

To address the challenge of accurate ride detection, we propose a ride detection system based on the GPS position of both the user and the train. Using the estimated distance between the user and the train, our system is able to accurately detect rides, even when they occur only between two stations.

The rest of this paper is organized as follows. First, we provide related works in Section II. Then, we introduce the overview of the gateless railway service in Section III. We detail the proposed method in Section IV and evaluates it by the simulation in Section V. In Section VI, we discuss the challenges to extend our approach to the real world. Finally, we summarize the conclusions in Section VII.

II. Related Work

Many studies in the previous decade have focused on inferring transportation modes based on GPS location. Some of them tried to infer the modes only from GPS trajectory data [2][7] while others tried to improve the accuracy of the inference by using additional information, such as accelerometer data [5] and GIS data [3][4][6]. However, all of them are not discussing the ride detection but are focusing on transportation mode detection.

As we mentioned in Section I, the main difference between the transportation mode detection and the ride detection is that high accuracy is required even for short GPS trajectories. When considering ride detection, it is necessary for fare charging to infer whether a user rode the train or not, even if they only rode it just for one station. However, previous studies and the criteria and features used in them tend not to account for such short GPS trajectories. Thus, applying them does not provide good enough accuracy of the inference in the ride detection.

For example, Stenneth et al. [3] proposed a machine learning approach using 8 features to infer the transportation

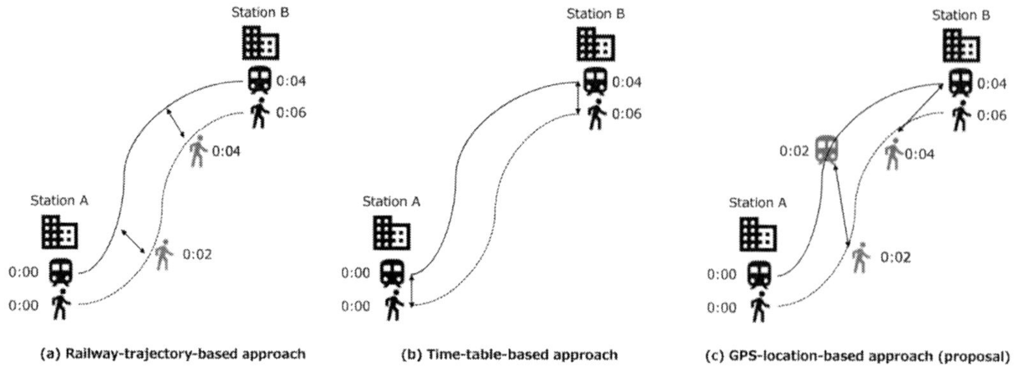

Figure 1. Comparison of railway ride detection

mode detection. In these features, the average distance between a user and a railway trajectory can be applied to the railway ride detection. Hereafter, we call the ride detection using this feature *railway-trajectory-based approach* in this paper. Figure 1(a) shows a conceptual diagram of the railway-trajectory-based approach. Since this approach does not consider the train's location but only uses the distance between a user and the closest railway line, decision errors might occur frequently if a road runs along the railway line, as the figure shows.

Montoya et al. [6] proposed an approach that considers the train location. They use station locations and timetables to distinguish train, subway, and tram in the transportation mode detection. More specifically, using route information in General Transit Feed Specification (GTFS) format provided by railway operators, they use the average distance between a user and stations on the route. In addition, they consider departure time and arrival time based on the timetable of the route. Hereafter, we call the ride detection using these criteria *timetable-based approach* in this paper. Figure 1(b) shows a conceptual diagram of the timetable-based approach. However, this approach has a limitation in the accuracy of the ride detection for short GPS trajectories since it does not consider the train location between stations.

To solve these challenges, we propose a *GPS-location-based approach* that uses GPS locations of both users and trains for the ride detection. Our proposed approach is based on the distance between the user and the train between two stations, based on their GPS locations. Figure 1(c) shows a conceptual diagram of GPS-location-based approach and its details are described in Section IV.

Note that Stenneth et al. [3] also use 2 features based on real-time bus locations but both of them are not appropriate for ride detection. One of them is Average Bus Closeness (ABC) that is the average distance between a user and the closest bus in a given time series, and the other one is Candidate Bus Closeness (CBC) that is the minimum value among the sums of the distance between a user and a bus at each time in a given time series. The former is a feature that mixes information regarding multiple buses and the latter is a feature that mixes information across the multiple bus stops. Thus, both of them cannot be used for ride detection.

III. Gateless Railway Service

This section describes the gateless railway service that our system could be used in. Figure 2 shows the overall architecture of the service.

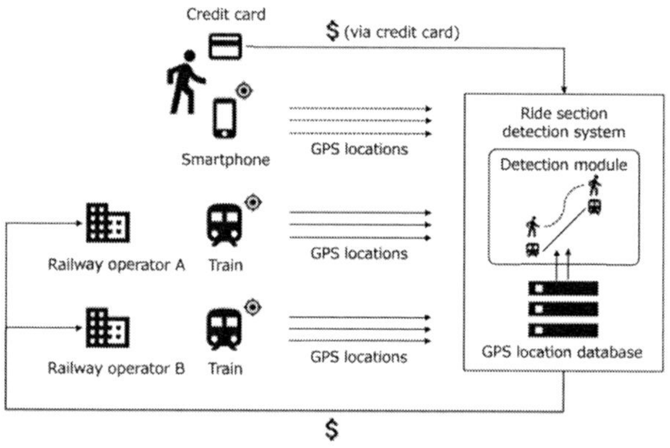

Figure 2. Gateless railway service architecture

In this gateless railway service, the ride detection system regularly collects GPS locations from user's devices, such as smartphones, and from trains operated by railway operators, and stores them in a database. The ride detection system periodically creates ride histories for each user and charges a user's credit card according to the histories. Then, the collected payments will be paid to the railway operators.

Introducing the gateless railway service which removes the gate itself has several advantages for both users and railway operators though smooth ticket examining using contactless smart cards have already been achieved in many countries. For users, the accessibility in stations will be drastically improved. For example, wheelchair users and people with strollers or big luggage can access platforms smoothly without minding the narrow gate. In addition, although a long queue can be formed at the time of congestion in main stations, the gateless railway service can alleviate it. As for railway operators, reducing costs for introducing and maintaining automatic ticket examining machines can be expected. Also, fare evasion in unmanned stations can be reduced if a fare control based on the degree of contribution for recording GPS locations as described in Section VI and sudden ticket examination is combined and performed.

IV. Railway Ride Detection

This section describes the proposed ride detection method. Let l_t^p and l_t^q be the location of a train p and a user q at a time t, respectively. We say that the user q is in *presumed ride state* for the train p if Euclidean distance d between l_t^p and l_t^q is less than or equal to the threshold θ_d.

Let $L^p_{(A,B)}$ be a sequence of the train p's location between stations A and B.

$$L^p_{(A,B)} = \{l_1^p, l_2^p, \cdots, l_n^p\} \quad (1)$$

where l_1^p is the train p's location at the departure time and l_n^p is the train p's location at the arrival time.

Similarly, a sequence of the user q's location at the same time can be represented as follows.

$$L^q = \{l_1^q, l_2^q, \cdots, l_n^q\} \quad (2)$$

We call the proportion of being the presumed ride state in n judgments *presumed ride rate* for the user q in $L^p_{(A,B)}$. We assume that the railway operators determine that the user virtually rode in the section and charge when the presumed ride rate is greater than or equal to a certain threshold.

V. EVALUATION

In this section, we evaluate our GPS location-based approach with respect to the accuracy of the ride detection by comparing it with the railway-trajectory-based one and the timetable-based one in a simulation. First, we describe the methodologies of the evaluation in Section V-A and then show the results in Section V-B.

A. Methodologies

1) Indicators: There are the following 4 patterns for the results of the inference.

- True Positive:
  Inferred virtually rode and actually rode.
- True Negative:
  Inferred not rode but actually not rode.
- False Positive:
  Inferred virtually rode but actually not rode.
- False Negative:
  Inferred not rode but actually rode.

We consider two indicators to evaluate the accuracy of the ride detection based on the number of each case above.

$$r_{FP} = \frac{N_{FP}}{N_{TN} + N_{FP}} \quad (3)$$

$$r_{FN} = \frac{N_{FN}}{N_{TP} + N_{FN}} \quad (4)$$

where r_{FP} is the false positive rate, r_{FN} is the false negative rate, and N_{TP}, N_{TF}, N_{FP}, N_{FN} are the numbers of true positives, true negatives, false positives, and false negatives respectively.

The false positive rate can be used to evaluate the possibility that users need to pay fare unreasonably and the false negative rate can be used to evaluate the possibility that railway operators will fail to collect the estimated fare. Of the two indicators, the false negative rate can be adjusted by changing the distance threshold θ_d, which is used for judging the presumed ride state. Thus, in this simulation, we evaluate the false positive rate by using the cases that can be misjudged as virtually rode.

TABLE I. RAILWAY OPERATORS AND EXAMPLES OF RAILWAY LINES

Railway operators	*Number of lines in the evaluation*	*Examples*
Odakyu	1	Odawara Line
Keio	7	Keio Line, Inokashira Line
Keikyu	1	Main Line
Seibu	2	Shinjuku Line, Ikebukuro Line
Tokyu	2	Toyoko Line, Denentoshi Line
TWR	1	Rinkai Line
Tobu	2	Isesaki Line, Tojo Line
JR East	34	Yamanote Line, Tokaido Line

2) Train Location: For the simulation, we use pseudo location information based on the railway trajectory data and the timetable data instead of the actual GPS location. MLIT in Japan provides GIS data, such as railway trajectories. Using the railway trajectories provided by MILT and the duration in timetables, we calculate the location of the train at a certain time. Specifically, assuming the train moves with a constant speed, we evenly divide the trajectory curve between stations by the distance moved at a fixed time interval (10 seconds in this evaluation).

3) User Location: We assume that a user travels between the target stations by car and unintentionally causes the misjudgment because the roadway often runs parallel nearby the railway line in urban areas of Japan. Specifically, we use the trajectory curve of the recommended drive route and its duration obtained by Google Maps Application Programming Interface (API). When calculating the location of the user, we assume that the car runs at a constant speed, for the simplicity.

4) Railway Lines: The targets are 50 lines and total 858 sections in the suburbs of Tokyo, Japan, which are operated by 8 railway operators. These 8 operators and example railway lines are shown in Table I. Note that we use one of the lines for the evaluation if an operator runs multiple lines in the same section. In addition, we exclude subway due to the difficulty of obtaining GPS locations but its detail will be discussed in Section VI.

B. Results

First, we compare the false positive rate between the railway-trajectory-based approach and our proposal while varying the threshold of the presumed ride rate and the distance (θ_d) in order to evaluate how the rate will be improved when considering the train position.

As shown in Table II, the proposed method provides a highly accurate false positive rate (about 1%) when lowering the presumed ride rate to 0.8 and raising the threshold of the distance to 150m.

On the other hand, in the railway-trajectory-based approach, misjudgments occurs in 5% of the sections even if the threshold of the distance is set to 50m. The false positive rate of the railway-trajectory-based approach may increase further in the real world situation since the length of the train is about 150-300m in general and railway operators would like to raise the threshold of the distance based on it in order to improve the false negative rate.

Next, we compare the false positive rate between the timetable-based approach and our proposal in order to evaluate how the rate will be improved when judging the position of

TABLE II. COMPARISON OF FALSE POSITIVE RATE WHETHER TRAIN POSITION IS CONSIDERED OR NOT

Threshold of presumed ride rate	*Threshold of distance (m)*	*Railway-trajectory-based*	*Proposal*
0.8	50	5.4%	0.0%
	100	17.0%	0.3%
	150	30.3%	1.0%
0.9	50	2.8%	0.0%
	100	10.8%	0.2%
	150	21.8%	0.8%
1.0	50	0.6%	0.0%
	100	5.2%	0.2%
	150	14.5%	0.6%

TABLE III. COMPARISON OF FALSE POSITIVE RATE WITH CONSIDERING TRAIN DELAY (THRESHOLD OF PRESUMED RIDE RATE ≥ 0.8)

Delay (sec)	*Threshold of distance (m)*	*Timetable-based*	*Proposal*
30	50	0.9%	0.1%
	100		0.6%
	150		2.4%
60	50	2.4%	0.0%
	100		1.2%
	150		4.1%
120	50	7.5%	0.0%
	100		1.9%
	150		5.6%

users and trains between stations in a fine-grained manner. Table III shows the results.

In this evaluation, since we assume the distance between the user and the departure/arrival station is zero, the timetable-based approach practically infers based on only the difference of the time duration between the user and the train. In other words, the false positive rate will vary only according to the tolerance for the time difference. For example, when using the low threshold of the time difference, the false positive rate will be improved but many false negative cases occur in the case of train delay. Thus, we vary the threshold of the time difference with 30, 60 and 120 seconds and we show the false positive rate of each case in Table III. Note that the rate in the case of the train delayed by 30, 60 and 120 seconds is shown for the proposed approach.

As shown in Table III, the proposed method can achieve good accuracy as a whole though it falls into a higher false positive rate than the timetable-based approach when using the large threshold of the distance.

VI. Discussion

In this paper, we propose a ride detection method based on the GPS locations in the gateless railway service. However, there are many challenges to be overcome in the production system.

A. *Radio Wave Dead Zones*

Applying our GPS-location-based approach to radio wave dead zones, such as subways and tunnels is a challenge. However, nowadays, mobile devices can receive radio waves even if they are in subways or tunnels and can infer the location according to the cellar base stations and WiFi access points. The accuracy is not high (e.g., a few kilometers), but we believe that it is possible to detect the ride section based on not only the GPS locations but also the data from other sensors, such as an accelerometer.

B. *Countermeasures for Fare Evasion*

Investigating the countermeasures for the fare evasion is also a challenge. As a simple way of the fare evasion, just turning off the power of the smartphone can be considered. Using faked GPS locations is also possible in some way. The former type of cheat can be reduced by introducing a fare control based on the degree of contribution for recording GPS locations. For example, offering some incentives by applying a higher fare if the GPS locations are intermittently lost may reduce the fare evasion. The latter type of cheat can be excluded by checking whether the operating system and/or the application is faked or not using API, such as SafetyNet in Android. However, the fare evasion cannot be detected if always turning off the power from the begining. Therefore, manual approaches, such as random control by service personnel and the expensive fine will be necessary.

VII. Conclusion

In this paper, we study ride detection based on GPS location as a new approach for implementing gateless railway service. Unlike the transportation mode detection, it is necessary for fare charging to detect the ride correctly even if the GPS trajectory is short. In order to achieve this, we proposed a ride detection method that uses criteria to evaluate how far the user and train were moving between two stations. In our simulation using railway line open data provided by MLIT in Japan, we show that our proposed method reduced false positives by 25%-100% in most cases.

We plan to develop a prototype and evaluate the proposed method with overall criteria including false negative error rate and efficacy of countermeasure for fraud prevention, such as incentive management by fare control.

Acknowledgment

The authors would like to thank Thomas Laurent for carefully proofreading the manuscript.

References

[1] Mitsubishi Electric Corporation, "Concepts for Advanced Rail Travel," 2017, URL: http://www.mitsubishielectric.com/news/2017/pdf/1120-a.pdf [accessed: 2019-02-01].

[2] Y. Zheng, Q. Li, Y. Chen, X. Xie, and W. Ma, "Understanding mobility based on gps data," in Proceedings of the 10th International Conference on Ubiquitous Computing (UbiComp 2008), 2008, pp. 312–321.

[3] L. Stenneth, O. Wolfson, P. S. Yu, and B. Xu, "Transportation mode detection using mobile phones and gis information," in Proceedings of the 19th ACM SIGSPATIAL International Conference on Advances in Geographic Information Systems, 2011, pp. 54–63.

[4] H. Gong, C. Chen, E. Bialostozky, and C. T. Lawson, "A GPS/GIS method for travel mode detection in New York City," Computers, Environment and Urban Systems, vol. 36, no. 2, 2012, pp. 131–139.

[5] P. Widhalm, P. Nitsche, and N. Brndie, "Transport mode detection with realistic smartphone sensor data," in Proceedings of the 21st International Conference on Pattern Recognition (ICPR2012), 2012, pp. 573–576.

[6] D. Montoya, S. Abiteboul, and P. Senellart, "Hup-me: Inferring and reconciling a timeline of user activity from rich smartphone data," in Proceedings of the 23rd SIGSPATIAL International Conference on Advances in Geographic Information Systems, 2015, pp. 62:1–62:4.

[7] Z. Xiao, Y. Wang, K. Fu, and F. Wu, "Identifying different transportation modes from trajectory data using tree-based ensemble classifiers," ISPRS International Journal of Geo-Information, vol. 6, no. 3, 2017, p. 57.

A Community Detection Algorithm Based on Granulation of Links

Samrat Gupta
Information Systems Department
Indian Institute of Management
Ahmedabad, India
e-mail: samratg@iima.ac.in

Pradeep Kumar
IT and Systems Department
Indian Institute of Management
Lucknow, India
e-mail: pradeepkumar@iiml.ac.in

Irina Perfilieva
Centre of Excellence IT4Innovations
University of Ostrava
Ostrava, Czech Republic
email: irina.perfilieva@osu.cz

Abstract—**The digital transformation of business and society has led to the growth of networks in almost every field. Finding communities in real world networks has been considered crucial for modern network science. Moreover, the organization of communities into co-occurring disjoint, nested and overlapping structures adds to the complexity of community detection problem. Therefore, methodological rigor is crucial for community detection so as to foster cumulative tradition in data and knowledge engineering. This paper proposes an algorithm for overlapping community detection based on the concepts of rough set theory. Initially, subsets of links are formed by using neighborhood links around each pair of nodes. Subsequently, we iteratively obtain the constrained linkage upper approximation of these subsets. The notion of mutual link reciprocity is used as a merging criterion during the iterations. The proposed algorithm is experimentally evaluated on eight real-world networks. Comparative analysis with state-of-the-art algorithms demonstrates the effectiveness of proposed algorithm.**

Keywords- community structure; clustering; rough sets; complex networks

I. INTRODUCTION

The technological advancement in contemporary digital world has led to the formation and mapping of systems which consist of many interconnected dynamical units. Such systems are collectively referred to as complex systems because their constituent units are capable of interacting not only with each other but also with the environment [1]. Some examples of complex systems include a social club that requires cooperation among its members to achieve a common goal, the Internet consisting of millions of interconnected routers and the human brain comprising millions of synaptically connected neurons [2]. All the networks arising from complex systems, irrespective of diversity in their origin, nature, size and scope, follow a common set of organizing principles [1]. Since the existence of cohesive subgroups (generally known as communities) is one of the fundamental properties of complex networks, identifying them is essential to explore and understand the dynamics of complex real-world systems.

Communities are considered as thickly connected subgroups of nodes within a complex network such that the link density within subgroups is much higher than the density of links between subgroups [3]. The dense inter-community connectedness exists due to organizational or functional components within a network such as groups of friends in a social network of students, and groups of companies with interlocking directorates in organizational networks [2]. In this research work, we design a community detection algorithm based on the unexplored theoretical synergy of the concepts of link communities in network science and upper approximation in rough set paradigm. As discussed in Section III, this synergy is constituted by expanding each link and its link neighborhood component using the concept of upper approximation rather than expanding each node and its node neighborhood component which has been the focus in prior research [4]-[7].

This paper is organized as follows. In Section II, we briefly present the motivation behind this work. In Section III, the methodology of the proposed algorithm is explained. Section IV presents the experimental setup. In Section V, the experimental results are discussed. Finally, Section VI concludes this work.

II. MOTIVATION

An effective community detection technique can transform business and society through its widespread applications. These applications range from topic detection in collaborative tagging systems, to event detection on social media content [3]. In the past, community detection techniques have been used to devise antiterrorism strategies and understand functional patterns of the human brain that can help in positioning and pricing of products [8][9].

Though researchers have been addressing the community detection problem for more than a decade, state-of-the-art algorithms still have several limitations [10]. A majority of the existing algorithms assign each node to only one community; some algorithms are domain specific; some require a priori knowledge about the number of communities; some are not scalable for large networks and some are unsusceptible to variations in size of communities. One of the major challenges encountered currently for community detection is the identification of overlapping communities which manifest the reality of today's world [11]. For instance, in social networks, individuals may belong to multiple communities due to their friendships, professional associations, family relationships and so on. Moreover, communities may overlap not only partially but also entirely such that one community is contained in another [12]. An effective community detection algorithm must be receptive to distinctive features of community structure in complex networks and be capable of detecting co-occurring disjoint, nested and overlapping communities.

III. LUAMCOM – PROPOSED ALGORITHM

Soft computing techniques for community detection such as evolutionary computing, swarm intelligence, fuzzy logic and genetic algorithms have gained popularity in recent years [13]-[15]. However, rough set theory has not been explored to its fullest potential for mathematical modelling of complex networks thus indicating methodological gaps in the burgeoning community detection literature.

The proposed Link Upper Approximation Method for COMmunity detection is abbreviated as LUAMCOM. Since, links are more idiosyncratic in nature as compared to nodes, pervasive overlaps in community structure are better discovered by clustering of links rather than nodes [16]. The proposed algorithm considers links of a complex network as entities to be clustered wherein each link and its neighborhood links form initial components (granule in rough set terminology) [17]. These initial components are termed as Link Neighborhood Subsets (LNS). Then, the concept of upper approximation is used iteratively to grow these components in a constrained manner until they merge to form stable components. This step consists of iterative formation of First Linkage Upper Approximation (FLUA) and Constrained Linkage Upper Approximation (CLUA) until convergence. The converged or stable components are actually the identified communities within a network. The notion of Mutual Link Reciprocity (MLR) is used as a merging criterion during the iterations. As shown in Figure 1, the iterative process followed by a fine-tuning process, ensures that the detected community structure displays high intra-community density of links, and low inter-community density of links. To the best of our knowledge, LUAMCOM is the first community detection algorithm based on integration of link granulation and upper approximation.

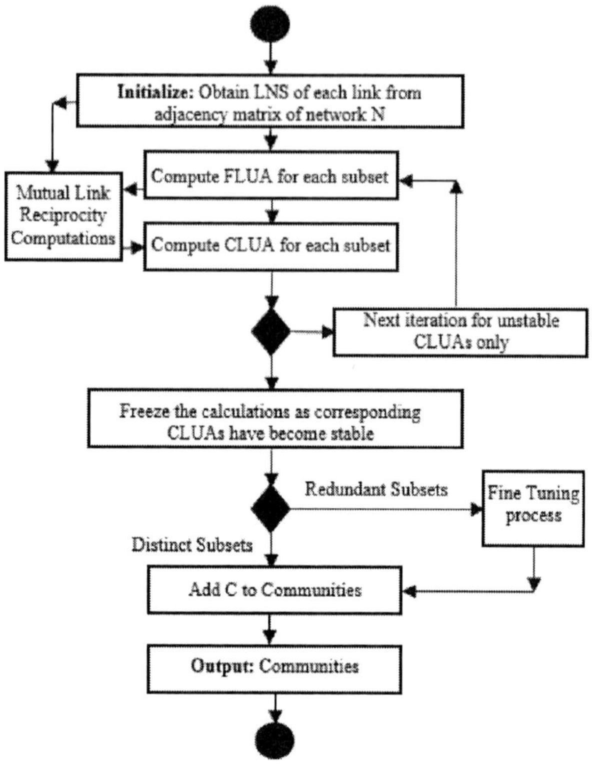

Figure 1. Flow Diagram of LUAMCOM

IV. EXPERIMENTAL SETUP

We conducted experiments on network datasets representing complex systems in diverse domains. These networks consist of a network of friendships at a karate club (34 nodes, 78 links) [18], network of bones in human skull (35 nodes, 79 links) [19], network of associations between dolphins (62 nodes, 159 links) [20], network of friendships in a high school (69 nodes, 220 links) [21], network of political books sold online by Amazon.com (105 nodes, 441 links) [22], co-appearance network of football teams (115 nodes, 613 links) [23], an online network of friendships on Facebook (2888 nodes, 2981 links) and a human protein-protein interaction network (3724 nodes, 8748 links) [24]. All the experimental work was conducted in the R programming environment. We used a system with Intel Core i5 processor and 8.00 GB RAM, running R version 3.2.5. The version 0.8.2 beta of Gephi software has been used for visualization.

To demonstrate the effectiveness of the proposed algorithm, we compare its performance with state-of-the-art community detection techniques using evaluation criteria na-mely Normalized Mutual Information (NMI) [25], partition density [16] and overlapping modularity [26]. Each of these evaluation measures has its own relevance and importance for measuring the quality of community detection. NMI computes the agreement between detected community structure and true community structure. In this work, we have used a variant of NMI that is designed especially for overlapping communities and results in the same NMI values as the standard measure when there is no overlap. Another measure used in this work is an extended version of modularity that can be used for evaluation of overlapping communities. This measure was proposed to address the limitations of traditional modularity. Finally, we have used a measure called partition to evaluate the quality of link based communities. Since partition density measures the intra-community density of links, it is considered more suitable for assessing the quality of overlapping community detection.

For comparison of the proposed algorithm with state-of-the-art algorithms, we consider the most relevant overlapping community detection algorithms such as Ahn Bagrow Lehmann (ABL) [16], Community Overlap PRopagation Algorithm (COPRA) [27], Clique Percolation Method (CPM) [28] and Greedy Clique Expansion (GCE) [29].

V. Experimental Results

The proposed algorithm identifies five overlapping communities in the human skull network. These five communities, generally known as *complexes* in case of biological networks include a complex representing the group of facial bones, groups of cranial bones, cervical bones, left and right ear ossicles bones. The overlapping community structure detected by the proposed algorithm in the human skull network is highly consistent with the results reported in existing literature [19] and shows the functional and developmental dependencies of bones in the human skull.

The proposed algorithm identifies five overlapping communities, one nested and one disjoint community in the high school network. The nested community within grade-9 corresponds to a subgroup of different ethnicity [21]. However, two nodes have been misclassified in the high school network. The proposed algorithm competes favorably with state-of-the-art community detection algorithms. Although the NMI value of GCE is slightly higher than that of the proposed algorithm, it detects only six communities and overlooks the nested community within grade-9 [21]. The overlapping nodes detected by the proposed algorithm are quite similar to existing overlapping community detection algorithms such as COPRA, GCE and ABL.

The experiment on karate club reveals two communities wherein all the nodes have been classified correctly. However, the proposed algorithm detects four nodes as overlapping, thus indicating evidence for dual memberships of some of the members within the karate club. This result is in accordance with the observation that some bridge nodes act as information carriers within the two communities of karate club [18]. The experiment on dolphin network divides the network into two communities consisting of 21 and 41 nodes without any misclassification. However, three overlapping sub-communities were found in the larger community. The composite performance of the proposed algorithm outperforms ABL, CPM and GCE on karate and dolphin networks. However, COPRA obtained higher score on the karate club network because of its higher NMI.

The proposed algorithm identifies three communities with one overlapping node on a network of political books (polbooks). The composite score of the proposed algorithm in the case of the polbooks network is higher than ABL, COPRA, CPM and almost equal to GCE. On the football network, the proposed algorithm identifies 11 communities and outperforms ABL, COPRA and CPM, while being slightly behind GCE in terms of composite score.

We also performed experiments on larger networks such as, a network of friendships extracted from Facebook and human protein interaction network downloaded from an online database [30]. In an undirected version Facebook network, 16 communities identified by the proposed algorithm were found to be structurally similar to those identified by the edge label propagation approach [24]. On the Protein Protein Interaction (PPI) network, the detected community structure was very similar to that of an algorithm based on binary tree theory [31].

VI. Conclusion and Future Work

In this paper, we proposed an algorithm based on granulation and upper approximation of links for overlapping community detection in complex networks. We have investigated the performance of the proposed algorithm on different types of networks. The proposed algorithm performs competitively with state-of-the-art community detection algorithms and effectively detects co-occurring disjoint, nested and overlapping community structures in complex real-world networks. While the proposed algorithm makes an important methodological contribution to the challenging problem of community detection, it is applicable only to undirected and unweighted networks. In the future, we intend to enhance the capability of the proposed methodology to detect communities in directed and weighted networks. We believe that the proposed algorithm will impart rigor while guiding future research in the field of complex network analysis.

References

[1] L. A. N. Amaral and J. M. Ottino, "Complex networks," The European Physical Journal B - Condensed Matter, vol. 38(2), 2004, pp. 147–162. doi: 10.1140/epjb/e2004-00110-5

[2] R. Albert and A.-L. Barabási, "Statistical mechanics of complex networks," Reviews of Modern Physics, vol. 74(1), 2002, pp. 47. doi: 10.1103/RevModPhys.74.47

[3] S. Papadopoulos, Y. Kompatsiaris, A. Vakali, and P. Spyridonos, "Community detection in Social Media: Performance and application considerations," Data Mining and Knowledge Discovery, vol. 24(3), 2012, pp. 515–554. doi :10.1007/s10618-011-0224-z

[4] P. Kumar, S. Gupta, and B. Bhasker, "An upper approximation based community detection algorithm for complex networks," Decision Support Systems, vol. 96, 2017, pp. 103-118. doi: 10.1016/j.dss.2017.02.010

[5] Z. Cui, W. Chu, and Y. Fu, "Community structure Detection Algorithm Based on Rough Set," In Second International Conference on Business Computing and Global Informatization (BCGIN), IEEE, 2012, pp. 533-536. doi: 10.1109/BCGIN.2012.145

[6] H. S. Cheraghchi, A. Zakerolhosseini, S. B. Shouraki, and E. Homayounvala, "A novel granular approach for detecting dynamic online communities in social network," Soft Computing, 2018, pp. 1-22. doi: 10.1007/s00500-018-3585-z

[7] A. Moayedikia, "Multi-objective community detection algorithm with node importance analysis in attributed networks," Applied Soft Computing, vol. 67, 2018, pp. 434-451. doi: 10.1016/j.asoc.2018.03.014

[8] U. K. Wiil, N. Memon, and P. Karampelas, "Detecting new trends in terrorist networks," International Conference on Advances in Social Network Analysis and Mining, IEEE, 2010, pp. 435–440. doi: 10.1109/ASONAM.2010.73

[9] M. T. De Schotten et al. "A lateralized brain network for visuospatial attention," Nature Neuroscience, vol. 14(10), 2011, pp. 1245–1246. doi: 10.1038/nn.2905

[10] W. Liu, M. Pellegrini, and X. Wang, "Detecting communities based on network topology," Scientific Reports, vol. 4, 2014. doi: 10.1038/srep05739

[11] J. Yang and J. Leskovec, "Overlapping community detection at scale: a nonnegative matrix factorization approach," The Sixth International Conference on Web Search and Data Mining, ACM, 2013, pp. 587–596. doi: 10.1145/2433396.2433471

[12] Z. Shi and A. B. Whinston, "Network Structure and Observational Learning: Evidence from a Location-Based Social Network," Journal

of Management Information Systems, vol. 30(2), 2013, pp. 185–212. doi: 10.2753/MIS0742-1222300207

[13] C. Shi, Y. Cai, D. Fu, Y. Dong, and B. Wu, "A link clustering based overlapping community detection algorithm," Data & Knowledge Engineering, vol. 87, 2013, pp. 394–404. doi: 10.1016/j.datak.2013.05.004

[14] T. Nepusz, A. Petróczi, L. Négyessy, and F. Bazsó, "Fuzzy communities and the concept of bridgeness in complex networks," Physical Review E, vol. 77(1), 2008. doi: 10.1103/PhysRevE.77.016107

[15] G. Jia et al. "Community detection in social and biological networks using differential evolution," In Learning and Intelligent Optimization, Springer, 2012, pp. 71–85. doi: 10.1007/978-3-642-34413-8_6

[16] Y. Y. Ahn, J. P. Bagrow, and S. Lehmann, "Link communities reveal multiscale complexity in networks," Nature, vol. 466(7307), 2010, pp. 761–764. doi: 10.1038/nature09182

[17] Z. Pawlak, "Rough sets," "International Journal of Computer & Information Sciences," vol. 11(5), 1982, pp. 341–356. doi: 10.1007/BF01001956

[18] W. W. Zachary, "An information flow model for conflict and fission in small groups," Journal of Anthropological Research, vol. 33(4), 1977, pp. 452–473. doi: 10.1086/jar.33.4.3629752

[19] B. Esteve-Altava, R. Diogo, C. Smith, J. C. Boughner, and D. Rasskin-Gutman, "Anatomical networks reveal the musculoskeletal modularity of the human head," Scientific Reports, vol. 5, 2015. doi: 10.1038/srep08298

[20] D. Lusseau et al. "The bottlenose dolphin community of Doubtful Sound features a large proportion of long-lasting associations," Behavioral Ecology and Sociobiology, vol. 54(4), 2003, pp. 396–405. doi: 10.1007/s00265-003-0651-y

[21] J. Xie, S. Kelley, and B. K. Szymanski, "Overlapping community detection in networks: The state-of-the-art and comparative study," ACM Computing Surveys, vol. 45(4), 2013, pp. 1–35. doi: 10.1145/2501654.2501657

[22] V. Krebs, "Books about US politics," http://www.orgnet.com, 2004 (accessed February 1, 2009).

[23] M. Girvan and M. E. Newman, "Community structure in social and biological networks," Proceedings of the National Academy of Sciences (PNAS), 2002, pp. 7821–7826. doi: 10.1073/pnas.122653799

[24] W. Liu, X., Jiang, M. Pellegrini, and X. Wang, "Discovering communities in complex networks by edge label propagation," Scientific Reports, vol. 6, 2016. doi: 10.1038/srep22470

[25] A. V. Esquivel and M. Rosvall, "Comparing network covers using mutual information,". arXiv Preprint arXiv:1202.0425, 2012.

[26] H. Shen, X. Cheng, K. Cai, and M.B. Hu, "Detect overlapping and hierarchical community structure in networks," Physica A: Statistical Mechanics and Its Applications, vol. 388(8), 2009, pp. 1706–1712. doi: 10.1016/j.physa.2008.12.021

[27] S. Gregory, "Finding overlapping communities in networks by label propagation," New Journal of Physics, vol. 12(10), 2010. doi:10.1088/1367-2630/12/10/103018

[28] G. Palla, I. Derényi, I. Farkas, and T. Vicsek, "Uncovering the overlapping community structure of complex networks in nature and society," Nature, vol. 435(7043), 2005, pp. 814–818. doi: 10.1038/nature03607

[29] C. Lee, F. Reid, A. McDaid, and N. Hurley, "Detecting highly overlapping community structure by greedy clique expansion," Proceedings of the 4th Workshop on Social Network Mining and Analysis, 2010, pp. 33–42.

[30] K. R. Brown and I. Jurisica, "Online Predicted Human Interaction Database. Bioinformatics," vol. 21(9), 2005, pp. 2076–2082. doi: 10.1093/bioinformatics/bti273

[31] Q. J. Jiao, Y. K. Zhang, L. N. Li, and H. B. Shen, "BinTree Seeking: A Novel Approach to Mine Both Bi-Sparse and Cohesive Modules in Protein Interaction Networks," PLoS ONE, vol. 6(11), 2011. doi: 10.1371/journal.pone.0027646

Towards Predictive Monitoring of Research Infrastructures

Jedrzej Rybicki
Juelich Supercomputing Center (JSC)
Juelich, Germany
Email: j.rybicki@fz-juelich.de

Abstract—**Nowadays, both modern computing infrastructures, as well as their scientific workloads exhibit far reaching complexity and diversity. Therefore, it is increasingly hard to comprehend and manage them in an efficient manner. In particular, it can lead to under- or overuse of resources. A prerequisite for efficient resource allocation is the ability to predict their usage. In this paper, we use real world workloads recorded in a modern research infrastructure to conduct load prediction. We use well established statistical model (ARIMA) and achieve good results in predictions. The big data challenge is here given not by the sheer size but rather by the speed of data collection and processing. The quicker the prediction is made, the more time is available for actions. Such predictions can be included in monitoring systems to give human operators better insights into the status of their infrastructures and lead to better load distribution.**

Keywords–Fast Data; Load prediction; Monitoring; Research infrastructures; Predictive model.

I. Introduction

This short paper marks the beginning of our research towards automatic monitoring and managing of distributed computing resources. Our main motivation stems from the increasing complexity of the distributed research infrastructures we have to manage. They comprise of High-Performance Computing (HPC), High-Throughput Computing (HTC), and Cloud resources. The resources are used by researchers from different disciplines cooperating across the borders to accomplish ambitious scientific goals. The usage patterns emerging from this far-reaching diversity are challenging for the underlying infrastructure. Yet, a mismatch in mapping of users demand on hardware resources may potentially result in high cost, low performance, and users' disappointment.

One of the prerequisites for an efficient resource allocation is the load prediction. Obviously, in case of increasing load more hardware resources need to be allocated, conversely decreasing load can trigger reallocation of idle resources. High and very high levels of load can also be an indicator that particular tasks were mapped on the wrong class of resources, e.g., Cloud nodes instead of HTC, and an adjusting action should take place. Given the fact that such an adjustment takes some time, it is of crucial meaning to predict the future demand directions to give the resource providers sufficient time for the required changes. Lastly, a sudden change of load can be an indication of a hardware failure or malicious action, potentially requiring human intervention. In this paper, we will examine if it is possible to predict future infrastructure workload based on the historical measurements.

Collecting and analyzing workload data is a challenging task. The single measurements are not large in size, but they are only meaningful if analyzed quickly. An application of decentralized approach for data evaluation would have clearly some interesting properties but our goal is to use existing monitoring infrastructure and extend it with a prediction capability. In this approach, data are collected locally and then transferred to the central unit for visualization, analysis, and storage.

Load analysis and prediction pave the way for an algorithm driven infrastructure, in which no operator intervention is required, but rather the infrastructure itself makes optimal usage of the available resources. Given the aforementioned complexity of the current research infrastructures, such an automatic, algorithm-driven support is not a fancy vision but rather an urgently required solution. It becomes increasingly hard for human operators to grasp the tendencies and problems in the managed infrastructures, and to make and implement reallocation decisions.

In this paper, we mainly focus on using the model for predicting future values of load in the test infrastructure. But a good model itself provides an insight in the underlying process which generated the experimental data. In our case, the model can potentially help us in understanding how the resources are used. This knowledge, in turn, can influence the choice of resources deployed and overall improve the quality of the service offered to the users.

The rest of the paper is structured as follows. In Section II, we shortly summarize some of the previous work on broadly defined predictions. Section III comprises our initial results. We provide information on our setup, analyze stationarity of the process we are going to predict on, and describe both the model used and its predictive performance. We conclude the paper with an outlook on future work in Section IV.

II. Related Work

There is some research done in the broad field of predictions that might be relevant and inspirational for our work. Amjady analyzed electric load to issue short term prediction of future load demand [1]. This is crucial for the economic and secure operation of power systems. There are some differences between electric load and hardware utilization, especially as the first one exhibits a strong seasonal component. Nevertheless, the existing body of work in this field provides meaningful insights into possibility and methodology of predictions, as well as their economic relevance.

Statistical Process Monitoring (SPM) using either statistics or machine learning methods can help in modeling and diagnosing of industrial process operations and production results [2]. The overarching goal here is to conduct preventive service before faults occur. The setting is similar to ours but the systems analyzed differ in many ways. The work, however, underpins the needs of algorithm help in managing complex infrastructures and again give valuable hints on methodology.

Roberts et al. [3] used profiles of power consumption to detect malware infections on the host machines. The deviation of recorded power consumption during predefined task were detected with kernel-based Support Vector Machines (SVM). The authors recorded four voltage and four corresponding current channels and achieved perfect detection of malware infections. Their problem statement differs substantially from ours, yet clearly shows the potential of analyzing CPU loads generated by applications.

Tao Li et al. [4] conducted a relevant study in a field similar to ours. They proposed an algorithm combining linear regression and the improved Knuth-Morris-Pratt match to predict the next moment load in the examined Cloud environment. Furthermore, they conducted initial studies on automatic Cloud resource reallocation based on this prediction. This work serves as a good comparison for our results as we use a slightly different setting and different predicting algorithm. Particularly, the authors used Cloud simulator for data generation whereas we use traces from real infrastructure. There exists also a more generic Patent by Wolters [5] on predictive monitoring of IT structures. It provides less technical details, but proves the commercial relevance of the work. There also exists a body of work which uses prediction for efficient scheduling of the computation jobs [6] [7]. The techniques used range from neuronal networks to statistical models with no clear favorite.

Our cross-disciplinary survey was intended to give us an overview on methodology used in different kinds of predictions. We have seen that techniques ranging from simple statistical models up to multi-layer neural networks are used. An open question is what method to use when predicting future values of a given feature. Artificial Neural Networks (ANNs), tend to perform well in some situations and fail in others. The question "Neural networks: Forecasting breakthrough or passing fad?" posed first by Chattfield [8] remains open. Thus, in this first attempt on the problem, we decided to stick to classical, and well-understood methods and explore the potential of the idea. In the future, work we might turn towards more sophisticated methods. However, there is some evidence that simple modeling methods tend to perform better than their more sophisticated counterparts [9]. We were also partly motivated by the need to better understanding of the process that generates the experimental data. Such an understanding is better achieved with simple models.

III. Evaluation

In our evaluation, we follow the well-established Box-Jenkins methodology [10]. In this approach, the analysis comprises of three phases: model identification, parameter estimation, and model checking.

A. *Data and tools*

For our experiments, we used data collected within our production infrastructure. It consists of a number of hosts offering different kinds of services for academic users. The services range from single-sign-on systems, through simple storage offerings, up to Grid-based computing end points. We use nagios [11] to perform periodic checks of the hosts and services running. The tests comprise of host reachability, disk usage, and relative CPU load, among others. Measurements were done over two days with 5 minutes frequency. For this initial evaluation, only load values were used.

TABLE I. STATIONARITY TESTS.

	Train	Test
Mean	0.0158	0.0183
Variance	0.0007	0.0008

The analysis was done with Jupyter Notebooks [12] and we used popular Python libraries like pandas [13], statsmodels [14], and matplotlib [15]. In this project, we follow the best practices for structuring data science projects [16].

B. *Model creation*

To model and predict load changes, we use a very popular Autoregressive Integrated Moving Average (ARIMA) model. In the identification phase, we check the applicability of the model. The first question that needs to be answered when analyzing time series, is the stationarity of the process. We used two metrics for that. Firstly, the series was split in a 60-40 ratio into parts which we later used for training and testing of the model. Then, both mean and variance for the two intervals were calculated. Only slight differences in values obtained for both intervals (see Table I), suggest the stationarity of the series. A more sophisticated way of establishing if a series is stationary is the Augmented Dickey–Fuller test [17]. The value calculated in the test was -3.611 laying beyond the 1% significance threshold (-3.441 in our case). Given the results of both tests, we can assume the series is close to stationary and proceed in model creation that should be able to predict future values. The small changes in the variance will be accounted for by differencing in the ARIMA process.

The ARIMA model is characterized by three parameters. The number of lags for autoregression is denoted as p. Parameter d defines the number of times the observations are differenced. Finally, the q parameter describes the size of the moving average window of the model. Since p basically defines the relationship between subsequent observations, a good hint for estimating its value is to use autocorrelation plot. On Figure 1, we can see that there is strong autocorrelation within the series, the first time the curve crosses 0 for lag 3, thus we take $p = 3$ in our model. Because the process seems to be close to stationary, we used a small value for $d = 2$. Finally, the remaining q was taken as 1, meaning that we perform, more or less exponential smoothing of the values, what makes sense for CPU loads. Furthermore, it is common to set at least one parameter value to one, as otherwise a risk of overfitting is high.

After fitting the model to data, we estimated its quality. The plot of model residuals distribution (Figure 2) shows that mean value of residuals is close to zero (0.381×10^{-3}) and the distribution is normal, confirming the good model fit.

C. *Prediction*

After successfully modeling the CPU load changes with ARIMA model, we tested how good it can predict the future values of load. This metric is crucial for the envisioned automatic steering of resource allocation. If the model is unable to predict correct values it would not be possible to account for them.

The predictions were made in a rolling manner. Firstly, we split the available data in two parts: train and test. The

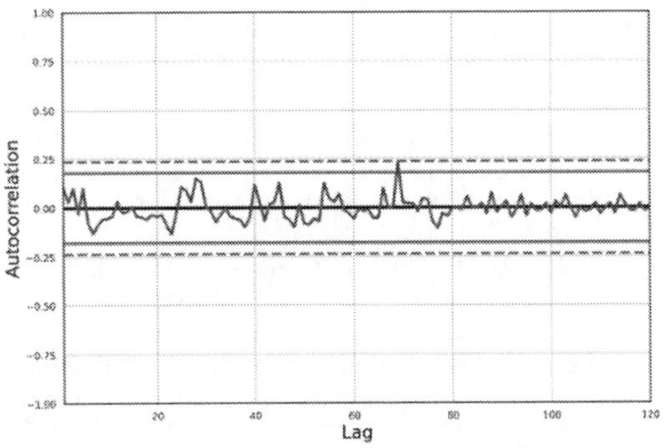

Figure 1. Autocorrelation plot of the measured CPU load.

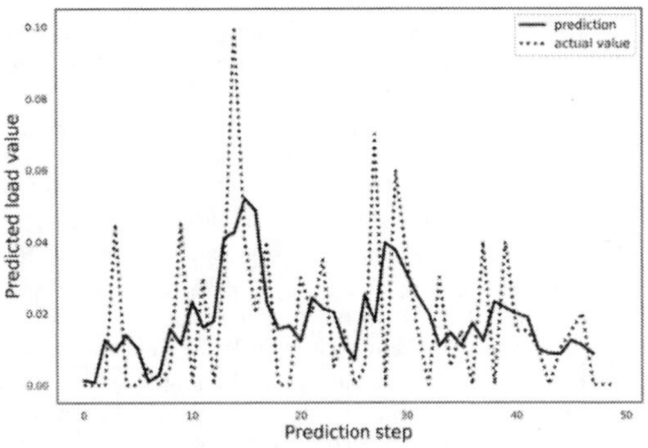

Figure 3. Predictions of CPU load made with the model.

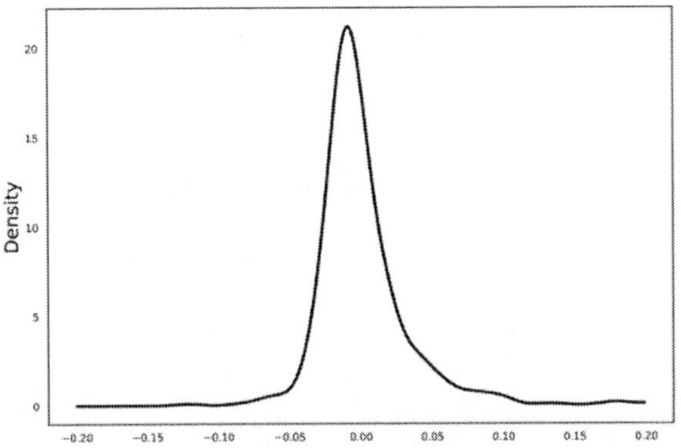

Figure 2. Distribution of model residuals.

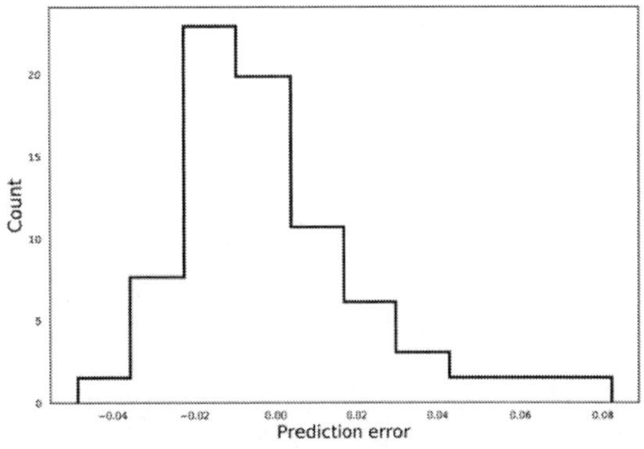

Figure 4. Distribution of prediction errors.

training set comprised of 350 measurements and was used to fit ARIMA model, with previously selected parameters $p = 3$, $d = 2$, and $q = 1$. Subsequently, a series of 40 predictions (corresponding to about 3.5 hour interval) were made. After each step, the predicted value was compared to the actual value from the test set. Finally, the model was retrained with the train set extended by the actual value. Figure 3 shows the quality of the predictions made by our model. The dashed line shows values from the test set, solid line represents predictions. One can see that the model is a little bit conservative and sluggish but overall predicts the values pretty well. The mean squared error of all predictions was 0.698×10^{-3}. Prediction error can be calculated as a difference between the actual and predicted value. The distribution of such an error is depicted on Figure 4. Most of the errors reside in the area close to 0.

IV. Conclusion and Future Work

In this paper, we modeled the utilization of an IT infrastructure and used this model to predict future changes in workload. The proposed model seems to be able to predict changes with acceptable accuracy. The results obtained in this initial study corroborate our assumptions and motivate us to further work on this subject.

Currently, we only used load values measured over time, but it will be interesting to see if other values available like disk or memory usage could help to improve the predictions. The data are available, but the current model cannot really deal with multidimensional data well. The straight-forward solution would be to use few ARIMA models to run in parallel and predict changes in each time series separately. Subsequently, the results would be combined to give a prediction of the holistic state of the resource.

Since our motivation is of a practical manner, we would like to integrate the model predictions into our infrastructure, monitoring solution. This will be the first step in assisting the human operators in grasping the tendencies in the managed infrastructure but also a field test for the proposed model.

References

[1] N. Amjady, "Short-term hourly load forecasting using time-series modeling with peak load estimation capability," IEEE Transactions on Power Systems, vol. 16, no. 4, Nov. 2001, pp. 798–805, ISSN: 0885-8950.

[2] S. J. Qin, "Survey on data-driven industrial process monitoring and diagnosis," Annual Reviews in Control, vol. 36, no. 2, 2012, pp. 220–234, ISSN: 1367-5788.

[3] R. A. Bridges, J. M. H. Jiménez, J. Nichols, K. Goseva-Popstojanova, and S. J. Prowell, "Towards malware detection via CPU power consumption: Data collection design and analytics," in Proceedings of 12th IEEE International Conference On Big Data Science And Engineering (TrustCom/BigDataSE), 2018, pp. 1680–1684, ISBN: 978-1-5386-4388-4.

[4] T. Li, J. Wang, W. Li, T. Xu, and Q. Qi, "Load prediction-based automatic scaling cloud computing," in Proceedings of International Conference on Networking and Network Applications (NaNA), Jul. 2016, pp. 330–335, ISBN: 978-1-4673-9803-9.

[5] T. J. Wolters, "Predictive monitoring and problem identification in an information technology (IT) infrastructure," Patent US7 107 339B1.

[6] H. Jiang, H. E, and M. Song, "Multi-prediction based scheduling for hybrid workloads in the cloud data center," Cluster Computing, vol. 21, no. 3, Sep. 2018, pp. 1607–1622, SSN: 1573-7543".

[7] X. Tang, X. Liao, J. Zheng, and X. Yang, "Energy efficient job scheduling with workload prediction on cloud data center," Cluster Computing, vol. 21, no. 3, 2018, pp. 1581–1593, ISSN: 1386-7857.

[8] C. Chatfield, "Neural networks: Forecasting breakthrough or passing fad?" International Journal of Forecasting, vol. 9, no. 1, 1993, pp. 1–3.

[9] K. C. Green and J. S. Armstrong, "Simple versus complex forecasting: The evidence," Journal of Business Research, vol. 68, no. 8, 2015, pp. 1678–1685, special Issue on Simple Versus Complex Forecasting.

[10] G. E. P. Box, G. M. Jenkins, G. C. Reinsel, and G. M. Ljung, Time Series Analysis: Forecasting and Control, ser. Holden-Day series in time series analysis and digital processing. Holden-Day, 1976, ISBN: 978-0-81621-104-3.

[11] W. Kocjan and P. Beltowski, Learning Nagios, 3rd ed. Packt Publishing, 2016, ISBN: 978-1-78588-595-2.

[12] Project Jupyter. [Online]. Available: https://jupyter.org/ [retrieved: Jan., 2019]

[13] pandas: Python data analysis library. [Online]. Available: http://pandas.pydata.org/ [retrieved: Jan., 2019]

[14] S. Seabold and J. Perktold, "Statsmodels: Econometric and statistical modeling with Python," in Proceedings of 9th Python in Science Conference, 2010, pp. 57–61, ISBN: 978-1-4583-4619-3.

[15] J. D. Hunter, "Matplotlib: A 2D graphics environment," Computing In Science & Engineering, vol. 9, no. 3, 2007, pp. 90–95.

[16] J. Rybicki, "Best practices in structuring data science projects," in Proceedings of 39th International Conference on Information Systems Architecture and Technology (ISAT). Springer International Publishing, 2019, pp. 348–357, ISBN: 978-3-319-99993-7.

[17] D. A. Dickey and W. A. Fuller, "Distribution of the estimators for autoregressive time series with a unit root," Journal of the American Statistical Association, vol. 74, no. 366a, 1979, pp. 427–431, ISSN: 0162-1459.

A Novel Methodology to Identify and Collect Data from Relevant Blogs Leveraging Multiple Social Media Platforms and Cyber Forensics

Tuja Khaund, Kiran Kumar Bandeli, Oluwaseun Walter, Nitin Agarwal
Department of Information Science
University of Arkansas at Little Rock
Little Rock, United States
e-mail: {txkhaund, kxbandeli, oxwalter, nxagarwal}@ualr.edu

Abstract—**Blogs play a vital role in retrieving real time information, a place for users to gain insights into events and also find communities with similar interests. However, being able to identify blogs that contain honest, unbiased opinion of individuals as opposed to biased or agenda-driven coverage, is quite a challenge. Secondly, blogs are notorious for being dynamic in structure, where their owner is entitled to give them a makeover whenever they want. This changing structure of blogs can be computationally expensive for researchers and Web crawlers. In this paper, we propose a methodology to help identify relevant blogs for specific events. We provide data statistics of a few real-world events where our methodology successfully identified relevant blogs and helped us study the information discourse. We then discuss the strengths and weaknesses of this methodology and highlight the best approach to crawling blogs.**

Keywords-blog; blog identification; relevant blogs; cyber forensics; unstructured data; social media; crawling.

I. INTRODUCTION

Social media is a gold mine of valuable resources that coordinate various real-life events to a wide audience. It allows people to voice their opinions, engage in discussions and share information. However, the Internet is built to follow the power law distribution where these sources usually get buried in the Long Tail. This makes social media a valuable source for event analysis studies and to identify quality sources from the pool of information is of utmost importance. A blog site or a blog is a collection of entries, called blog posts, by individuals displayed in reverse chronological order. These posts are a combination of text, images, and Uniform Resource Locators (URL), which direct to other blogs and/or to other Web pages. Blogging has become a popular means for mass Web users to express, communicate, share, collaborate, debate, and reflect [1].

Generally, a blog has different posts written by either a single author or multiple authors on topics of interest or on events happening around the world. While blogs allow free medium to write on any events or issues, some authors use this for spreading mis/disinformation. Some of the studies on blogs look at various events such as European Union (EU) migrant crisis to analyze shift in narratives regarding migrants [2], Venezuelan Socio-Economic Crisis to gain situational awareness of the protests [3], role of blogs in disinformation campaign coordination [4], and events related to fake news in Baltic States spreading misinformation [5].

In this paper, we propose a methodology to identify relevant blogs for specific events. We use different input streams, which will obtain URLs for blog identification such as streaming Twitter based on geo-location, using Cyber Forensic analysis to detect blogs based on Google Analytics tracking codes, etc. Google Analytics tracking code monitors the activity of a website and provides insights about visitors of the website. The Analytics tracking code may be added directly to the Hypertext Markup Language (HTML) code of each page on a website, or indirectly using a tag management system such as Google Tag Manager.

The rest of the paper is organized as follows. Section II describes the related work. Section III depicts the methodology used to identify blogs from various sources. Section IV discusses the analysis and findings obtained from the methodology. We discuss the challenges to this research in Section V and conclude with intended future work in Section VI.

II. LITERATURE REVIEW

The blogosphere has generated a vast amount of content over the years making it difficult to keep track of all the resources. Identifying rich and legitimate sources of information is a challenge every researcher is trying to overcome with new methods and models. Mahata et al. [6] applied an evolutionary mutual reinforcement model to identify and rank highly 'specific' social media sources and 'close' entities related to an event. Agarwal et al [7] studied sentiments and opinions of people towards public and political events from blogs. Twitter [8][9] and YouTube [10] have been extensively used to analyze information dissemination during natural disasters and crisis. Event related contents have been found leveraging the tagging and location information associated with the photos shared on Flickr [11]. Becker et al. [12] studied how to identify events and high quality sources related to them from Twitter. In order to identify the genuine sources of information, credibility and trustworthiness of event related information were studied from Twitter [13]. New methods were investigated for filtering and assessing the variety of sources obtained from social media for journalists [14]. All these works try to explore the quality of information, in terms of relevancy, usefulness, timeliness of the content and usage patterns of authoritative users producing the content. However, only a few works involved the blogosphere. Our work will help researchers find a new direction in identifying blogs from credible sources and validate them.

III. METHODOLOGY

Our methodology highlights two major categories of blog data collection. First, we identify blogs and then conduct a relevance assessment to obtain the most relevant blogs. The first phase of this methodology may generate noise and also contain content from mainstream media. The main motive is to obtain rich, unbiased opinions of users to study the information discourse during crucial real-world events. The high-level design of the methodology is illustrated in Figure 1.

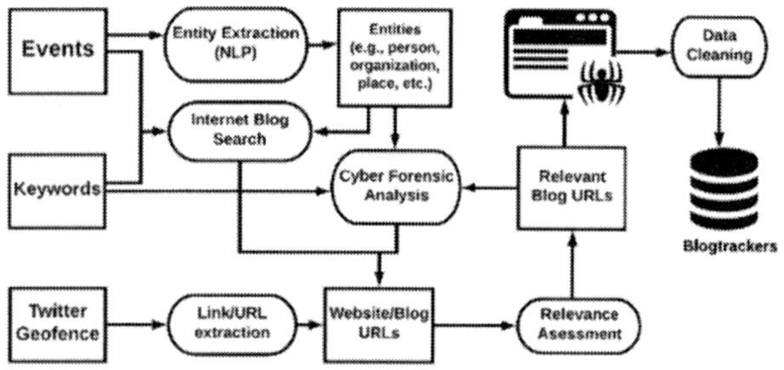

Figure 1. Blog identification and collection methodology.

Data is injected from multiple streams into the engine. The proposed methodology is scalable, meaning more such data streams can be added as they become available. The 'Events' data stream focuses mainly on local events of the country or region of interest, such as Ukraine while studying their Parliamentary Affairs, Europe while analyzing the migrant crisis, etc. The 'Keywords' data stream comprises of information provided to us by domain experts such as names of Parliament members, local political groups etc. The 'Twitter Geofence' data stream extracts tweets based on geolocation. Another laborious approach exists where data is collected from Facebook, where we analyze content dissemination based on keywords or trending topics for events of interest. Each data stream has a different shared engine that enables us to extract entities, run cyber forensic analysis and extract more blogs using a snowball approach. After we have exhausted every possible stream, we run checks for relevant content. This process is tedious but the results are promising. The relevant blogs are then crawled, cleaned and stored in our database. We provide a step-by-step procedure of the data streams used in the methodology below.

A. *Blog Identification*

The most important step to our methodology is to identify blogs.

1) *Event Analysis:*

In this process, we refer to our case study of Ukraine's Parliament Affairs where we study public discourse on social media platforms, mainly blogs. There are four different steps in this blog identification process.

a) We begin by searching for the presence of Ukrainian bloggers and blogs on the Web and different social media platforms such as Twitter, Facebook, etc., using keywords such as 'Ukraine bloggers' 'Poroschenko', 'war Donbass', 'Verkhovna Rada', 'Ukraine blog', 'Petro Poroshenko Bloc', 'People's Front', etc.

b) We then create an event dictionary using popular news website like 'Kyivpost.com' and 'Unian.info' as Ukrainian event sources. We also keep a record of keywords used by these sources for our next step.

c) We use keywords from the event dictionary to search for blog sites on social media platforms, google search engine, and these 2 websites 'searchblogspot.com' and 'search.wordpress.com'.

d) Finally, we find other relevant blogs from blogrolls of already identified blogs.

It is also important to note that converting the keywords to Ukrainian language, while searching for blogs, enabled us to discover more blogs that are specific to Ukraine. The keywords chosen are subjective but we seek guidance from domain experts for better results.

2) *Twitter Daily Dumps:*

There are four steps involved in this process of blog identification.

a) We set up a geofence based on coordinates of a particular country or region of interest and stream Twitter for daily tweets. The results are stored as JavaScript Object Notation (JSON) files.

b) We extract all the URLs from our Twitter daily dump and also expand all the shortened URLs.

c) We filter all the unique hyperlinks based on keywords such as 'blog', 'blogspot', 'wordpress' etc. and extract the domains (of blogs).

d) Finally, we perform relevance checks on the filtered blogs and add them to the crawling pipeline.

This methodology extracts every tweet that has been posted within the set geo-coordinates and at times, extracts noise. As a result, we run cyber forensic analysis on these blogs to discard irrelevant URLs.

3) *Cyber Forensics:*

There are four steps to this blog identification process.

a) Once we identify blogs from the Twitter daily dumps, we run these blogs through a cyber-forensic analysis tool, Maltego [1], to extract more blogs.

b) These blogs are identified based on common Google Analytics tracker codes.

c) External hyperlinks (out-links) are also extracted from these blogs and then, we proceed to conduct the relevance assessment.

d) Finally, relevant blogs are then added to the crawling pipeline and then stored in the database for further analysis.

This analysis can be snowballed until we have no more blogs left to identify, as shown in Figure 1.

B. Relevance Assessment

Identifying relevant blogs is a manual process where blogs are distributed among members of the team. This process is subjective; team members know exactly which keywords to choose in order to detect data streams delivering the most promising results. The criteria include keywords that are relevant to the events. For example, while studying the blog discourse of Ukraine, we focused on keywords such as 'Ukraine',. names of parliament members, discussion of bills being passed or introduced into the legislation, etc. We were able to detect more relevant blogs from the Event Analysis and Cyber Forensics data streams. We try to eliminate content posted on mainstream media such as news sites, etc. to minimize bias. We analyze the blog's content and the links shared in it. Also, we rate a blog's severity as low, medium or high based on their content.

This methodology is open, scalable and expandable based on the number of data streams available. In order to improve the scalability of the effort, information retrieval-based relevance checks are conducted with keywords provided by domain experts. In the next section, we provide statistics of blog identification obtained for various events.

IV. ANALYSIS AND FINDINGS

A. Data Statistics

Using the methodology proposed in Section III, we have crawled 108 blog sites, at the time of writing this paper and more blogs are queued for crawling. Blogs that have been crawled are from the following datasets – The North Atlantic Treaty Organization (NATO) Trident Juncture Exercise 2018, migrant crisis in the EU, and Venezuelan Socio-Economic Crisis. Below we provide detailed statistics for each source:

1) NATO Trident Juncture Exercise 2018:

NATO's Trident Juncture exercise 2018 that happened during the period Oct. 2018 and Nov. 2018, in Norway has caused an increase in the anti NATO narratives on blogs. This sentiment was also observed during various exercises conducted by NATO (such as, Trident Juncture 2015, Brilliant Jump 2016, and Anakonda 2016). Using the methodology presented in Figure 1, we identified 46 blogs that had anti-NATO propaganda discourse. Figure 2 and Figure 3 demonstrates the statistics about this dataset.

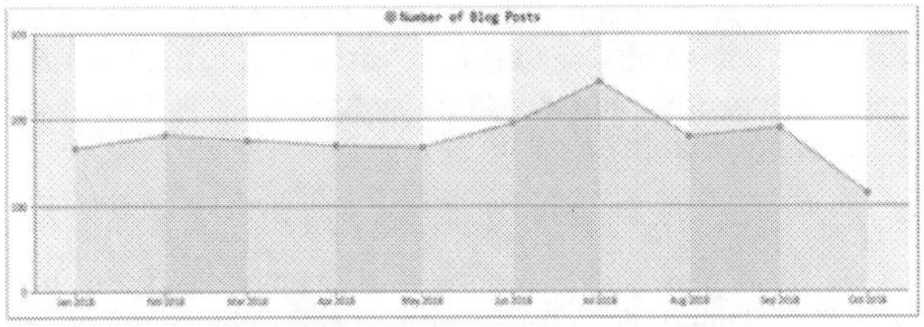

Figure 2. Blog post distribution of Anti-NATO blogs.

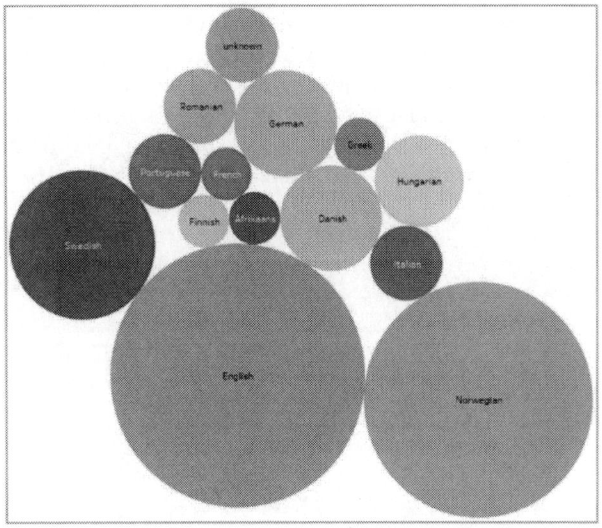

Figure 3. Language distribution of Anti-NATO blogs

2) EU Migrant Crisis:

Due to the conflict in Eastern Europe and Middle East during late 2015 and 2016, many people were migrating from war torn regions to stable regions in Europe. This dataset was collected in early 2016 during the peak time of migrant crisis in Europe. Figure 4 and Figure 5 provide the details of the dataset.

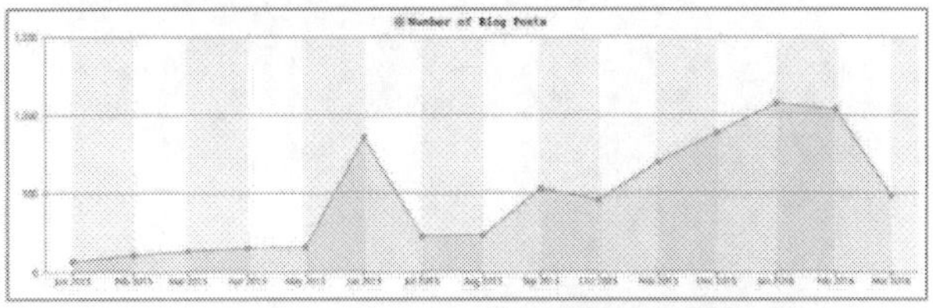

Figure 4. Blog post distribution of EU Migrant Crisis blogs.

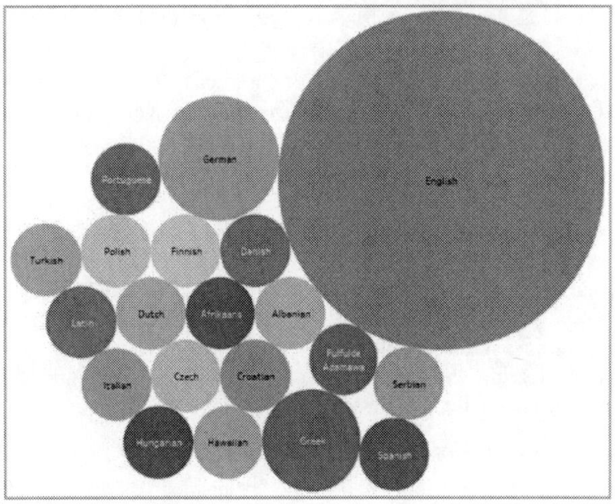

Figure 5. Language distribution of EU Migrant Crisis blogs.

3) Venezuelan Socio-Economic Crisis:

To analyze the socio-economic crisis in Venezuela from blogosphere, we collected data mainly for the period of mid-2016 and early 2017. During this period, many protests occurred covering the crisis event. Figure 6 and Figure 7 provide details about this dataset.

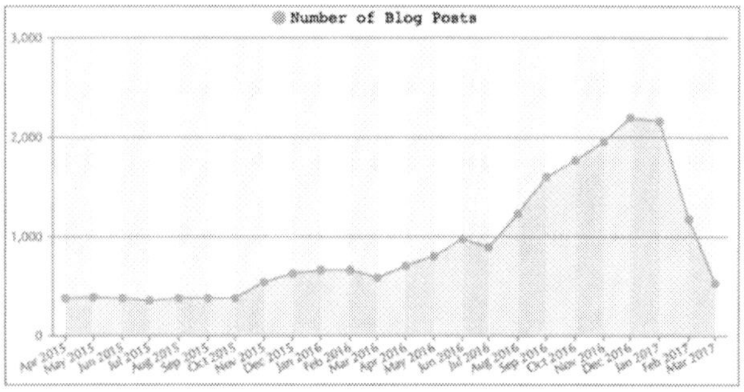

Figure 6. Blog post distribution of Venezuelan Socio-Economic Crisis blogs.

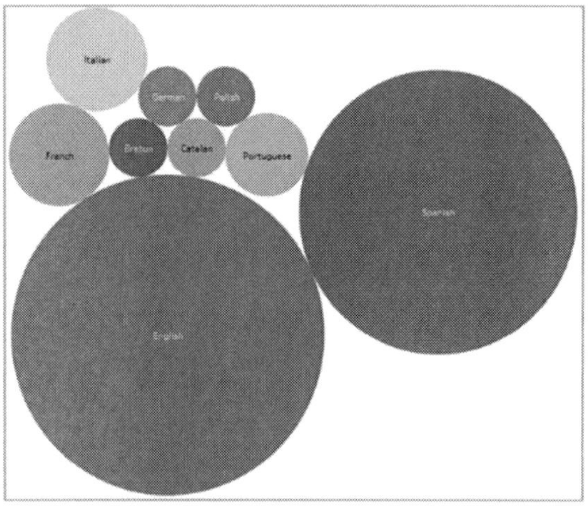

Figure 7. Language distribution of Venezuelan Socio-Economic Crisis blogs.

The analysis was conducted for three case studies that used the methodology. This is to show that we were able to get results based on the tasks listed on our methodology.

V. DISCUSSION

This paper presents a methodology, which will help researchers identify blogs. The semi-automated tasks will enable a user to obtain a much richer and prominent set of blogs, which otherwise will be extremely difficult given the dynamic nature of blog structure. However, blog identification and collection is a laborious task and has numerous challenges throughout the stages.

A. Challenges of identifying relevant blogs

The major portion of the relevance assessment is performed manually, which, in itself, is a challenge. But there exists a series of hurdles underlying the process of blog assessment.

1) Noise: Keyword-based blog searches often yields unexpected results. Blogs are not genre specific and may contain posts about world affairs, travelling, food, etc.

2) Limited Availability: A few blogs that were discovered have fewer blog posts (less than 10), while others no longer publish blog posts and a few others moved to different websites. Additionally, the content of these blog posts may or may not discuss the subject matter of interest.

3) Separating Blogs and News: During the initial stages of this methodology, differentiating blogs from mainstream websites became difficult because of the way these websites are structured.

4) Mainstream Dominance: Majority of Web links identified through search engines and social media sites were mainstream websites.

B. Challenges of blog data collection

A few challenges encountered during blog collection include the following:

1) Application Programming Interface (API) restriction: Various tools such as: BlogPulse [15], Blogdex [16], and Technorati [17], etc., were previously available to analyze blog data, but these efforts have been discontinued. As a result, there is no API available to extract blog data.

2) Dynamic blog structure: Dealing with blogs is similar to working with a moving target. Blog site owners are entitled to make changes to their blog structure any time. This confuses a trained Web crawler as it was formerly instructed to follow one structure, which has now been altered. As a result, the entire effort of blog crawling needs to be repeated for the new structure of blog site. Additionally, each blog requires its own parser to crawl the data.

3) Noise: Irrespective of how well a crawler is trained, noise is always crawled. Social media plugins (such as Facebook share plugins, Twitter share plugins, etc.) and advertisements from the blog site could be crawled as JavaScript.

4) No standardization: While we collect blog data, we parse important attributes for analysis. Once such attribute is date. While extracting the date field from blog posts, we noticed that it differs in format from blog site to blog site. In other words, a single standard is not followed in these blogs.

5) No automation: The process of blog crawling is not fully automated. Even the most intelligent/careful parsing may capture some noise. Manual intervention is required to identify and eliminate noise.

VI. CONCLUSION

In this paper, we proposed a methodology to help identify relevant blogs for specific events. We provided data statistics of a few real-world events where our methodology successfully identified relevant blogs and helped us study the information discourse. We then discussed the strengths and weaknesses of this methodology and highlighted the best approach to crawling blogs.

Conducting relevance assessment was a challenging task during this research is since it was performed manually. This is the most important task in our methodology because it helps us detect credible and important data sources. Automating this process will not only save a lot of time, but it will make blog crawling more scalable. We have tested a few blog sites that are hosted on WordPress and results are acceptable. We would like to extend this task to other blogs as a future work.

ACKNOWLEDGMENT

This research is funded in part by the U.S. National Science Foundation (IIS-1636933, ACI-1429160, and IIS-1110868), U.S. Office of Naval Research (N00014-10-1-0091, N00014-14-1-0489, N00014-15-P-1187, N00014-16-1-2016, N00014-16-1-2412, N00014-17-1-2605, N00014-17-1-2675), U.S. Air Force Research Lab, U.S. Army Research Office (W911NF-16-1-0189), U.S. Defense Advanced Research Projects Agency (W31P4Q-17-C-0059), the Jerry L. Maulden/Entergy Endowment at the University of Arkansas at Little Rock and Arkansas Research Alliance. Any opinions, findings, and conclusions or recommendations expressed in this material are those of the authors and do not necessarily reflect the views of the funding organizations. The researchers gratefully acknowledge their support.

REFERENCES

[1] M. N. Hussain, A. Obadimu, K. K. Bandeli, M. Nooman, S. Al-khateeb, and N. Agarwal, *A Framework for Blog Data Collection: Challenges and Opportunities*. June, 2017.

[2] M. N. Hussain, K. K. Bandeli, S. Al-khateeb, and N. Agarwal, "Analyzing Shift in Narratives Regarding Migrants in Europe via Blogosphere," 2018.

[3] E. L. Mead, M. N. Hussain, M. Nooman, S. Al-khateeb, and N. Agarwal, "Assessing Situation Awareness through Blogosphere: A Case Study on Venezuelan Socio-Political Crisis and the Migrant Influx."

[4] N. Agarwal and K. K. Bandeli, "Examining Strategic Integration of Social Media Platforms In Disinformation Campaign Coordination," *Def. Strateg. Commun.*

[5] N. Agarwal and K. K. Bandeli, "Blogs, Fake News, and Information Activities," in *Digital Hydra: Security Implications of False Information Online*, NATO Strategic Communications Center of Excellence (StratCom COE), 2017, pp. 31–45.

[6] D. Mahata and N. Agarwal, "What does everybody know? identifying event-specific sources from social media," in *Computational Aspects of Social Networks (CASoN), 2012 Fourth International Conference on*, 2012, pp. 63–68.

[7] N. Agarwal, H. Liu, J. Salerno, and S. Sundarajan, "Understanding group interaction in blogosphere: a case study," in *Proc 2nd international conference on computational cultural dynamics (ICCCD), September*, 2008, pp. 15–16.

[8] T. Khaund, S. Al-Khateeb, S. Tokdemir, and N. Agarwal, "Analyzing Social Bots and Their Coordination During Natural Disasters," in *International Conference on Social Computing, Behavioral-Cultural Modeling and Prediction and Behavior Representation in Modeling and Simulation*, 2018, pp. 207–212.

[9] F. Cheong and C. Cheong, "Social media data mining: A social network analysis of tweets during the Australian 2010-2011 floods," in *15th Pacific Asia Conference on Information Systems (PACIS)*, 2011, pp. 1–16.

[10] M. N. Hussain, S. Tokdemir, N. Agarwal, and S. Al-Khateeb, "Analyzing Disinformation and Crowd Manipulation Tactics on YouTube," in *2018 IEEE/ACM International Conference on Advances in Social Networks Analysis and Mining (ASONAM)*, 2018, pp. 1092–1095.

[11] T. Rattenbury, N. Good, and M. Naaman, "Towards automatic extraction of event and place semantics from flickr tags," in *Proceedings of the 30th annual international ACM SIGIR conference on Research and development in information retrieval*, 2007, pp. 103–110.

[12] H. Becker, M. Naaman, and L. Gravano, "Selecting Quality Twitter Content for Events." *ICWSM*, vol. 11, 2011.

[13] M. Gupta, P. Zhao, and J. Han, "Evaluating event credibility on Twitter," in *Proceedings of the 2012 SIAM International Conference on Data Mining*, 2012, pp. 153–164.

[14] N. Diakopoulos, M. De Choudhury, and M. Naaman, "Finding and assessing social media information sources in the context of journalism," in *Proceedings of the SIGCHI Conference on Human Factors in Computing Systems*, 2012, pp. 2451–2460.

[15] N. Glance, M. Hurst, and T. Tomokiyo, "BlogPulse: Automated Trend Discovery for Weblogs," in *WWW 2004 workshop on the weblogging ecosystem: Aggregation, analysis and dynamics*, New York, NY, USA, 2004, vol. 2004.

[16] C. Marlow, "Audience, structure and authority in the weblog community," p. 9.

[17] D. Sifry, "State of the blogosphere 2007," 2008.

Efficient Qualitative Method for Matching Subjects with Multiple Controls

Hung-Jui Chang
Department of Applied Mathematics
Chung Yuan Christian University,
Taoyung, Taiwan
Email: hjc@cycu.edu.tw

Yu-Hsuan Hsu, Chih-Wen Hsueh
Department of Computer Science and Information Engineering,
National Taiwan University,
Taipei, Taiwan
Email: {b99902110, cwhsueh}@csie.ntu.edu.tw

Tsan-sheng Hsu*
Institute of Information Science, Academia Sinica,
Taipei, Taiwan
Email: tshsu@iis.sinica.edu.tw
*Corresponding Author

***Abstract*—In the era of learning healthcare systems and big data, observational studies play a vital role to discover hidden (causal) associations in the dataset. To control bias, a matching step is usually employed to match case subjects to control candidates in observational studies randomly. The matching ratio refers to the number of control candidates matched with one case subject, and the successful matching rate is the percentage a matching is found given a matching ratio. A good matching algorithm should be not only efficient but also have high successful matching rate and high quality of randomness which means that a control candidate has a roughly equal chance of being matched with any of the matchable study cases. In this paper, we propose a matching algorithm, which is efficient with above mentioned good properties, RandFlow, a high-quality matching algorithm, is proposed and compared with commonly used ones - Simple_Match, Matchit, and Optmatch. The benchmark testing shows the effectiveness of the new algorithm. In our experimental studies, we noticed that the variation of the estimated Relative Risk (RR) value is minimized at the maximum matching ratio. Thus, we propose a two-phase matching method to obtain more reliable study results. The first phase is to identify the maximum matching ratio, and followed by matching multiple times and then take an average.**

Keywords–matching; observational study; relative entropy

I. INTRODUCTION

Observational studies are often used for investigating causal relationships. Given two events, α and β, researchers can analyze whether the occurrence probability of the event β is affected by the event α happening previously. In the medical field, an event can be a diagnosis, prescription or treatment. To control bias, several approaches have been applied, and one of them is matching [1]. Hence, the observational study process starts from identifying the study group G_α (those individuals with α), matching to the control candidates $G_{\neq\alpha}$ (those individuals without α), and then performing statistical analysis to draw a conclusion. For example, Relative Risk (RR) is used to estimate the relative risk of having β with and without the occurrence of α before. For example, in Table I, there are $a+b$ individuals with the event α, and a of them also with the event β. The conditional probability, R_1, which denotes the probability of having β under the condition of with the event α is therefore $a/(a+b)$. Also, there are $c+d$ individuals without the event α, and c of them with the event β. The conditional probability, R_2, which denotes the probability of having β under the condition of without α is therefore $c/(c+d)$. The RR value is defined as $RR = R_1/R_2$. RR values greater than, less than, or equal to 1 indicate positive, negative or no relationships, respectively. Other statistics, such as Odds Ratio (OR), may be used instead of RR depending on the study design.

TABLE I. EXAMPLE OF STUDY GROUP AND ITS MATCHED CONTROL GROUP

	α	$\neg\alpha$
β	a	c
$\neg\beta$	b	d
Sum	$a+b$	$c+d$

Matching is a critical step in the analysis of the observational study. Generally, a matching algorithm randomly permutes the order of the input of study case s, and control candidate c, and then checks whether the input s-c pair can be matched, and finally matches s with K-fold eligible controls one by one. The constant K is called the matching ratio. Some matching methods assign a propensity score to each pair [2] and return a matching with the best total score. However, if the distribution of cases is skewed, the study case may not be able to match with the required amount of controls successfully and would be dropped to avoid incurring further bias. Therefore, the output matching needs to satisfy some quality criteria, such as randomness and successful matching rate. In a good quality matching algorithm, a control candidate has a roughly equal chance of being matched with any of the matchable study cases. Keeping as many successful matchings as possible is also desired.

There are some commonly used matching methods, like Simple_Match [3], MatchIt [4][5], and Optmatch [6]. The former is based on a simple randomized greedy approach using SAS and the randomized algorithm has no proof of being able to deliver a matching in reasonable time in [3], and the latter two are variations of the well-known max flow algorithm [7] though with a performance guarantee, but does not consider any randomness. If the matching is only performed once with a small matching ratio, the result may not be stable in the sense that it is possible that different matchings may yield fluctuating statistics, such as RR or OR. To obtain a reliable result, it is better to match multiple times and take an average of all the outcomes. However, it is not practical to do repeated matching due to its heavy time consumption. Moreover, determining the matching ratio is also a cloudy issue in practice. In the past few decades, the case-control study has been suggested to match with four or five times of controls [8]. It was reported that "beyond a ratio of about 4/1, little power improvement results from increasing the number of controls" [9]. However, a matching ratio of 10 or even 15 is also seen in some studies [10][11]. In Hennessy's study [12], they indicated a higher matching ratio might be needed while the disease prevalence is low and hence, the implied matching ratio should be data dependent [13]. Up to date, few studies are investigating the issue of finding a good matching ratio.

Previous researches have focused on the impact of the matching ratio [13], and whether to use a matching or not [14]. But how to determine the matching ratio is less discussed. To resolve the above problems, we proposed a high-quality matching algorithm called *RandFlow*, which adopts the idea from maximum flow in graph theory. In RandFlow, we added some vital functions to raise the randomness and matching efficiency. Furthermore, we leveraged the high efficiency of RandFlow to determine the optimal matching ratio. By using RandFlow, the maximum matching ratio of each data set is calculated, and the range of the suitable matching ratio is also determined. The researcher can choose a preferred matching ratio according to the suggested range.

The remainders of this paper is organized as follows. In Section II, we describe our matching algorithm, the data source used in this study and the factors compared between different matching methods. In Section III, we show the experiment results of RandFlow and the comparison between RandFlow and the original methods. In Section IV, we discuss the comparison results and summarized our conclusions.

II. METHODS

The approach of our method is to formulate our problem in the well-known framework of flows in networks [7]. Hence, our methods come with performance and correctness guarantees. In this study, we used Taiwan's National Health Insurance Research Database (NHIRD) [15] as a data source and examined the validity of RandFlow by three causal relations reported in the published papers. We then compared RandFlow with the above matching methods with regard to successful matching rates, RR values and quality of randomness.

A. RandFlow Algorithm

We transform the matching problem in Figure 1(a) to the well-known max flow problem [7] in Figure 1(b). In a max flow problem, we assign maximum integer weights, not exceeding the pre-assigned capacity, to the edges so that for each vertex other than the source and sink, the sum of weights on its incoming edges equals the sum of weights on its outgoing edges. A study case S_i is matched with those control candidates C_j so that the weight of the edge from S_i to C_j is 1. The outcome is called a *max flow*. We further require that each study case has the same sum of incoming edge weights, which is called the *maximum matching ratio*, denoted by r. Thus, each study is matched with exactly r candidates, and each candidate is matched at most once. Since a max flow is found, r is as large as possible. Note that the value of r is data dependent. Each data set has its own maximum matching ratio. Naturally, it is unreasonable to ask for a matching whose ratio is more than r. In addition to whether a matching of a specified size can be found efficiently or not, we also concern whether the resulting matching is random or not, i.e., whether each candidate has an equal chance of being selected by any case subject. Without considering constraints incurred from competitions between case subjects, we use the well-known *entropy* [16] E of the ideal distribution among all possible candidates that can be matched to a case subject. Then we measure the entropy E' of the actual distribution of candidates being found by applying the matching repeatedly says 1000 times. We define the *relative entropy* to be $\frac{E'}{E}$ to quantify the quality of randomness in the matching obtained.

There are known algorithms to find such a max flow in $O(|E||F|)$ time, where E is the set of edges and F, called *flow*, is set of edges with weight 1 between the study cases and candidates. The value of $|F|$ is the number of edges inside. The algorithm finds a maximum flow by finding successively what is called an *augmenting flow* F' so that each time F' increases the current flow value by 1 after canceling edges from S_i to C_j and from C_j to S_i at the same time. We extend the original algorithm by finding a random augmenting flow, instead of a fixed one using a Randomized version of Depth First Search (RDFS). We also use a merging technique so that given two candidates C_i and C_j are merged if they have incoming edges from the same set of study cases. We also randomly shuffle the ordering of study cases from the input to obtain better randomness quality. Our revised algorithm runs faster and uses less memory than the original one in practice. The technical details can refer to our technique report [17].

B. Data source

The NHIRD is a nationwide database extracted from the claim data of the National Health Insurance (NHI) program in Taiwan for research purposes. In recent years, NHIRD has been widely used to identify potential causal relationships. This study also used NHIRD as the data source and which was reviewed by the Institutional Review Board of Academia Sinica, Taiwan (approval number: AS-IRB-BM-16043). As a benchmark, we selected three distinct causal relations from two published papers. One paper investigated the bidirectional relationship between Obstructive Sleep Apnea (OSA) and depression [18]. The study showed a positive relationship that patients with OSA have increased the risk of occurring depression, and vice versa. The other paper examined whether previous Statin use in patients with stroke affects the subsequent risk of dementia [19]. The study found a negative relationship in such a way that Statin use in patients with stroke decreases the risk of dementia. In this study, we define an event pair as the former event affects the occurrence of the following event. Hence, the relationship between depression and subsequent OSA is denoted as Event Pair I, and the reverse is Event Pair II. The relationship between

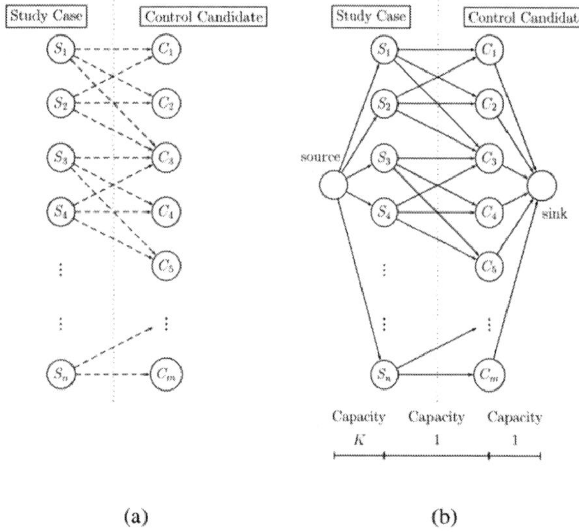

Figure 1. An example of transforming the matching problem into a flow problem.

Statin use in patients with stroke and following dementia is Event Pair III.

C. Comparisons between matching methods

In the original studies, event pair I and II were performed by exact match. Among these two event pairs, each study case was matched with five controls. Regarding event pair III, each study case was matched with one control by propensity score match [20] instead. In our study, all experiments were done by exact match. We used the ratio of control candidates to study cases to conjecture the maximum matching ratio.

We then compared the matching methods with regard to successful matching rates, RR values and quality of randomness. Successful matching rate is defined as the percentage of matched study cases that are not dropped. We assessed the average execution time, the corresponding successful matching rates and RR values with matching ratios from 1 to 30 (to 90 in the case of Event Pair II). To further understand the variation of RR values, we also examined the standard deviation of RR, R_1, and R_2. R_1 and R_2 represents the risk of having in the study group (G_α) and control group ($G_{\neq\alpha}$), respectively. The ratio of R_1/R_2 is RR. For the quality of randomness, we calculated the relative entropy of the matched control candidates with three different matching ratios: 70%, 100% and 110% of the maximum matching ratio. RR value and relative entropy were run 100 times and took the average. Because the programs implemented in C are more efficient and memory saving, we only compare C implementations in terms of successful matching rates, RR value and quality of randomness. All the experiments were performed on a Ubuntu 14.04 system with an Intel(R) Core(TM) i7-3770 CPU 3.40 GHz, and 16 Gbytes RAM.

III. Results

A. General result of the randomly sampled data

Figure 2 shows the result of the randomly generated data. The x-axis denotes the real RR value, and the y-axis denotes the estimated RR value which is calculated by RandFlow. Each point in the figure represents one data set. The results show RandFlow can get an estimated RR value very close to the real RR value. The statistic results are summarized in Table II. The first and second column denotes the real RR value and the estimated RR value. The third to fifth column denotes the absolute error between the real and the estimated RR value, the variance of the estimated RR value and the standard deviation of the estimated RR value. The experiment results show the absolute error RandFlow Algorithm is less than 0.06 and the variance and standard deviation is only 0.10 and 0.33, respectively.

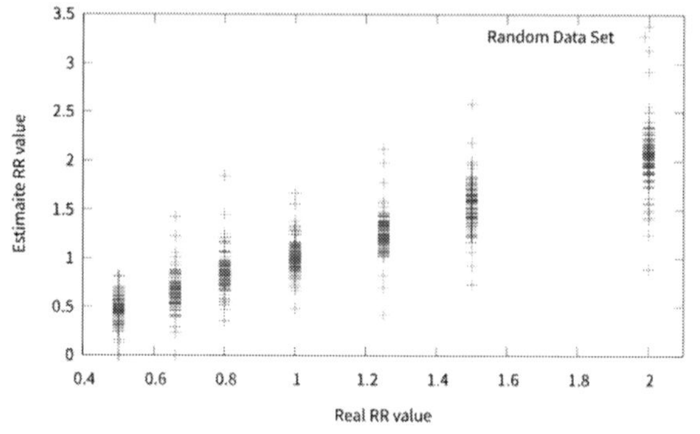

Figure 2. The distribution of real RR value and the estimated RR value of RandFlow.

TABLE II. THE STATISTIC RESULTS OF REAL RR VALUE AND THE ESTIMATED RR VALUE OF RANDFLOW.

Real RR	Estimated RR	Δ	Variance	STD
0.50 (1/2)	0.462	0.038	0.021	0.144
0.66 (2/3)	0.658	0.002	0.033	0.182
0.80 (4/5)	0.854	0.054	0.041	0.202
1.00 (1/1)	1.016	0.016	0.029	0.169
1.25 (5/4)	1.259	0.009	0.049	0.209
1.50 (3/2)	1.542	0.042	0.056	0.236
2.00 (2/1)	2.049	0.049	0.105	0.325

B. General information of the selected event pairs

Table III shows the general information of the selected event pairs from the original papers and our results, including the number of controls/control candidates, the ratio of control candidates to study cases, and maximum matching ratio.

TABLE III. GENERAL INFORMATION OF THE SELECTED EVENT PAIRS.

	Event Pair I	Event Pair II	Event Pair III
Original results			
No. study cases	27,073	6,427	5,527
No. control cases	135,365	32,135	5,527
Matching ratio	5	5	1
Our results			
No. control candidates	562,707	619,904	9,102
Control candidates/Study cases	≈21	≈97	≈2
Maximum matching ratio	11	51	0
Total edge	149,676,628	38,629,676	404,835

Among these event pairs, the greatest number of study cases was found in Event Pair I. With such a great amount of study cases, there were a total of more than 149 million edges generated while matching by RandFlow. We speculated the maximum matching ratio would be different among the event pairs as it turned out to be the ratio of 11, 51 and zero for Event Pair I, II and III, respectively. Additionally, these event pairs covered both positive and negative relationships. As a result, we believed that they could be representatives for testing matching quality.

C. RR values and Successful matching rates

Flow-based matching methods keep on matching until they use up all the matchable control candidates. They are expected to have the same traits in terms of RR value variation and successful matching rate. Hence, we only show the comparisons between Simple_Match and RandFlow in this section.

Overall, the average RR values of Simple_Match are higher than the values of RandFlow. In both methods, the average RR values are fairly stable while the matching ratio is small and gradually decrease when the matching ratio exceeds a certain value. In RandFlow, the decline occurs at the maximum matching ratio. By contrast, the decline of Simple_Match happens earlier than that (Figure 3(a) and 3(b)). In the case of a negative relationship in Event Pair III, the average RR values increase instead of decrease (Figure 3(c)).

Generally speaking, the variation of RR values of Simple_Match are more unstable than that of RandFlow. In both methods, the variation of RR values steadily decrease and then turn up at a certain matching ratio. The least variation of RR values of RandFlow occurs right at the maximum matching ratio. That of Simple_Match happens before the maximum matching ratio (Figure 3(d)-3(f)).

Since RR is calculated as R_1 divided by R_2, we examined the variation of R_1 and R_2 in RandFlow to further survey where the RR variation comes from. When the matching ratio is less than the maximum matching ratio, no study cases are dropped; thus, the standard deviation of R_1 remains zero. On the other hand, the standard deviation of R_2 decreases with matching ratio until it reaches the maximum. When the size of the control group increases to a certain number, the standard deviation of R_2 becomes relatively small and steady. Beyond the maximum, the standard deviation of R_1 surges because study cases are dropped rapidly (Figure 3(g)-3(i)).

Figure 4 shows the comparison of successful matching rates between Simple_Match and RandFlow. Because Simple_Match is based on a simple greedy algorithm, the matching results from it may vary. We used both the minimal (Simple_min) and the maximal (Simple_max) results from the 100 trials for comparison. Whether the minimal or the maximal result from Simple_Match, the successful matching rates drop before the maximum matching ratio, whereas that of RandFlow remains 100%. At any fixed matching ratio, RandFlow has the highest successful matching rates. Although Simple_Match runs faster than RandFlow, when the execution time is fixed, it cannot achieve the successful matching rate of RandFlow.

D. Quality of randomness

Optmatch and Matchit are both flow-based matching methods without randomly shuffling the input graph. In other words, their matched results remain unchangeable and no randomness at all. By contrast, we implemented RandFlow with inputting random graph and RDFS to enhance the quality of randomness. In this section, we show the comparison of the quality of randomness between RandFlow and Simple_Match.

Figure 5 shows that Randflow has a better quality of randomness than Simple_Match. Relative entropies of Event Pair I and II were tested at 70%, 100% and 110% of the maximum matching ratio in 100 trials. The relative entropy of RandFlow was estimated to be around 1 and generally higher than that of Simple_Match. Additionally, RandFlow has consistently stable entropy at any matching ratio and study case. Even if the ratio was set at 110% of the maximum matching ratio, the relative entropy of Randflow slightly decrease. For those study cases having small sets of control candidates, that of Randflow remains high. By contrast, the relative entropy of Simple_Match fluctuates widely as the matching ratio increases. For those study cases having less matchable control candidates, that of Simple_Match plunges.

IV. Discussion

In this study, we adopted maximum flow theory to develop a highly efficient and good-quality matching method, RandFlow, for matching subjects with multiple controls. This method can accomplish difficult matching tasks, like matching 20 thousand study cases to 30 times controls within a few seconds. Comparing with the most popular matching method, RandFlow has a good quality of randomness and finds a matching rather than drops study cases as long as such a matching exists. Matching is used to make the study cases and controls to have similar distributions across confounding variables. During the matching process, the controls are expected to be randomly selected from the control candidates. Anything that may affect the sampling design like dropping cases should be avoided. Our study used relative entropy to quantify randomness and then verified that RandFlow has a good quality of randomness. The randomness of RandFlow does not vary with the chosen matching ratios as it is no more than the maximum ratio. With regards to successful matching rate, RandFlow outperforms simple greedy algorithms due to the nature of algorithms. Overall, RandFlow surpasses those commonly used matching methods.

Matching ratio is data dependent and should be differentially set at the maximum matching ratio to obtain consistent results. In the past few decades, the case-control study has been suggested to match with four or five times of controls. Previous studies had indicated a higher matching ratio may be desired [9][12][13]. Beyond the previous studies, we tested three distinct data sets and performed matching multiple times at a range of matching ratios. In our experiments, we found that the maximum matching ratio varies with the input data set and the least variation of RR values always happens when we set the matching ratio to be the maximum. This can be explained from the perspective of graph theory. If the matching ratio requested h is no more than the maximum matching ratio w, then we have many possible different matchings. From the law of large number, the RR value calculated from many instances is stable and close to the real average case. If h is more than w, then we do not have many choices in selecting the pairings. The deviation of RR computed tends to be higher than the formal case. Therefore, rather than using an empirical

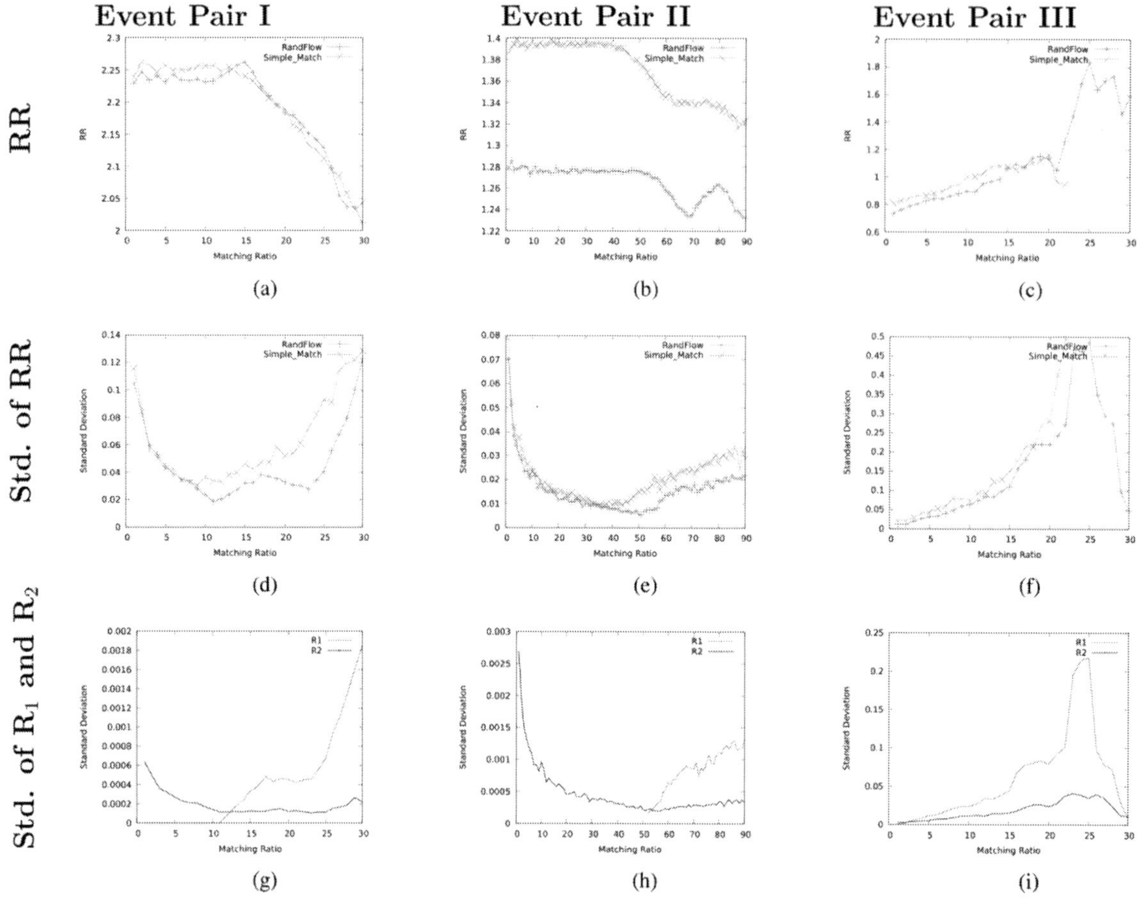

Figure 3. RR values and standard deviation of RR, R_1 and R_2 of Simple_Match and RandFlow.

fixed matching ratio, we suggest matching each study at its maximum matching ratio multiple times and taking an average for consistent results.

RandFlow being an exact matching has an inherent limitation. Of being unable to match some study cases with the required amount of controls while the distribution of the confounding variable is skewed. In the extreme case, even 1:1 match cannot be reached; thus, the RR values will be unstable at any matching ratios. In these circumstances, other matching methods should be considered in order to obtain reliable results.

In this study, we developed a highly efficient matching method and demonstrated its good quality of randomness. From our experiments, we further conclude that the matching ratio is data dependent and should be differentially set at the maximum matching ratio. For future study, we suggest that matching should be done in two phases. The first phase is to identify the maximum matching ratio. Then, the second phase is to carry out matching using the maximum matching ratio several times and take an average statistics. Using a two-phase matching, researchers can obtain stable results and draw unbiased study conclusions accordingly.

Acknowledgment

This work was supported in part by MOST, Taiwan, Grant No. 104-2221-E-001-021-MY3 and Multidisciplinary Health Cloud Research Program: Technology Development and Application of Big Health Data. Academia Sinica, Taipei, Taiwan. The authors would like to thank Mei-Lien Pan, Hsiao-Mei Tsao and Da-Wei Wang for their useful comments for the paper writing and proofreading.

References

[1] E. A. Stuart, "Matching methods for causal inference: A review and a look forward," Statistical science: a review journal of the Institute of Mathematical Statistics, vol. 25, no. 1, 2010, p. 1.

[2] P. R. Rosenbaum and D. B. Rubin, "Constructing a control group using multivariate matched sampling methods that incorporate the propensity score," The American Statistician, vol. 39, no. 1, 1985, pp. 33–38.

[3] H. Kawabata, M. Tran, and P. Hines, "Using SAS® to match cases for case control studies," in Proceeding of the Twenty-Ninth Annual SAS® Users Group International Conference, vol. 29, 2004, pp. 173–29.

[4] D. E. Ho, K. Imai, G. King, and E. A. Stuart, "Matching as nonparametric preprocessing for reducing model dependence in parametric causal inference," Political analysis, vol. 15, no. 3, 2007, pp. 199–236.

[5] ——, "Matchit: Nonparametric preprocessing for parametric causal inference," Journal of Statistical Software, 2007, pp. 1–28.

[6] B. B. Hansen, "Full matching in an observational study of coaching for the SAT," Journal of the American Statistical Association, vol. 99, no. 467, 2004, pp. 609–618.

[7] L. R. Ford Jr. and D. R. Fulkerson, "Maximal flow through a network," Canadian journal of Mathematics, vol. 8, no. 3, 1956, pp. 399–404.

[8] S. Wacholder, D. T. Silverman, J. K. McLaughlin, and J. S. Mandel, "Selection of controls in case-control studies: Iii. design options," American journal of epidemiology, vol. 135, no. 9, 1992, pp. 1042–1050.

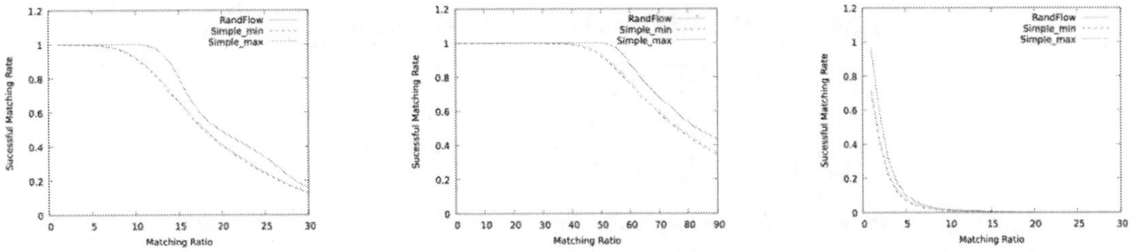

(a) Event Pair I (b) Event Pair II (c) Event Pair III

Figure 4. Successful matching rate of Simple_Match and RandFlow. Simple_min and Simple_max represent the minimal and maximal matching rate from the 100 trials run by Simple_Match.

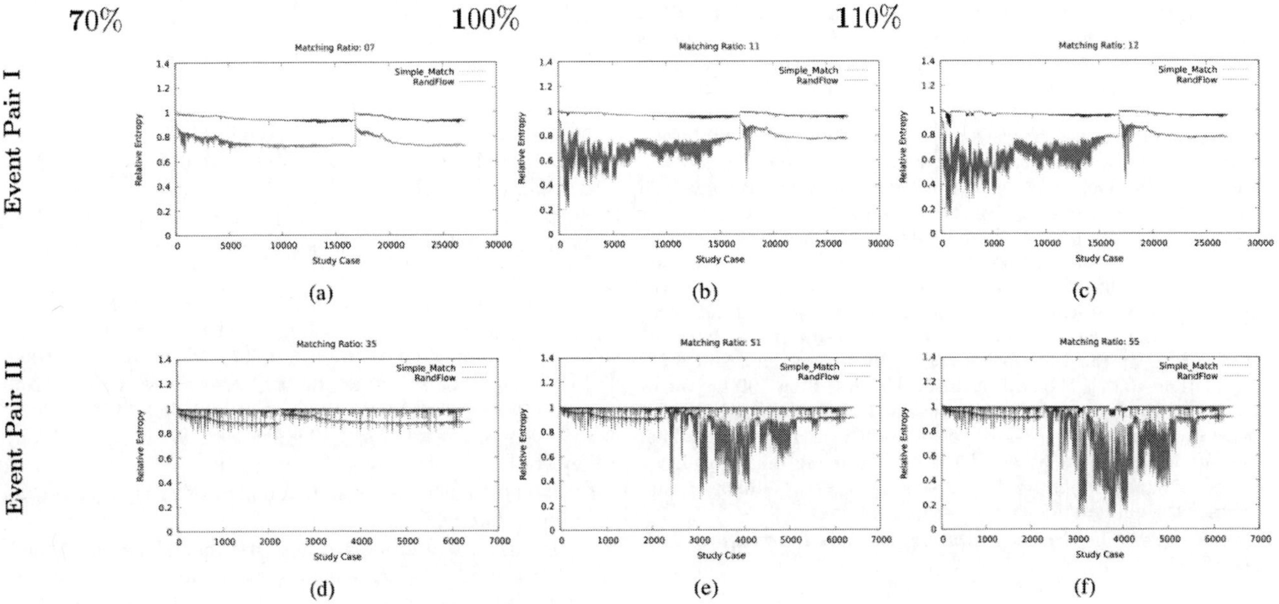

Figure 5. Relative entropy of Simple_Match and RandFlow in Event Pair I, II.

[9] D. A. Grimes and K. F. Schulz, "Compared to what? finding controls for case-control studies," The Lancet, vol. 365, no. 9468, 2005, pp. 1429–1433.

[10] M.-L. Pan, L.-R. Chen, H.-M. Tsao, and K.-H. Chen, "Relationship between polycystic ovarian syndrome and subsequent gestational diabetes mellitus: a nationwide population-based study," PloS one, vol. 10, no. 10, 2015, p. e0140544.

[11] K.-J. Tien et al., "Obstructive sleep apnea and the risk of atopic dermatitis: A population-based case control study," PloS one, vol. 9, no. 2, 2014, p. e89656.

[12] S. Hennessy, W. B. Bilker, J. A. Berlin, and B. L. Strom, "Factors influencing the optimal control-to-case ratio in matched case-control studies," American Journal of Epidemiology, vol. 149, no. 2, 1999, pp. 195–197.

[13] K. J. Rothman, S. Greenland, and T. L. Lash, Modern epidemiology. Lippincott Williams & Wilkins, 2008.

[14] T. Faresjö and Å. Faresjö, "To match or not to match in epidemiological studiesxsame outcome but less power," International journal of environmental research and public health, vol. 7, no. 1, 2010, pp. 325–332.

[15] "National health insurance research database, Taiwan , National Health Insurance Administration, Ministry of Health and Welfare, Taiwan, R.O.C." retrieved: February, 2019. [Online]. Available: http://nhird.nhri.org.tw/en/index.htm

[16] C. E. Shannon, "A mathematical theory of communication," ACM SIGMOBILE Mobile Computing and Communications Review, vol. 5, no. 1, 2001, pp. 3–55.

[17] H.-J. Chang, Y.-H. Hsu, C.-W. Hsueh, and T.-S. Hsu, "Efficient randomized algorithms for large-scaled exact matching with multiple controls: Implementation and applications," Institution of Information Science, Academia Sinica, Taiwan, Tech. Rep. TR-IIS-17-005, 2017.

[18] M.-L. Pan et al., "Bidirectional association between obstructive sleep apnea and depression: A population-based longitudinal study," Medicine, vol. 95, no. 37, 2016, p. e4833.

[19] M.-L. Pan, C.-C. Hsu, Y.-M. Chen, H.-K. Yu, and G.-C. Hu, "Statin use and the risk of dementia in patients with stroke: A nationwide population-based cohort study," Journal of Stroke and Cerebrovascular Diseases, 2018.

[20] L. S. Parsons, "Reducing bias in a propensity score matched-pair sample using greedy matching techniques," vol. 26, 01 2001, pp. 214–226.

Creating Data-Driven Ontologies
An Agriculture Use Case

Maaike H.T. de Boer and Jack P.C. Verhoosel

Data Science department, TNO (Netherlands Organisation for Applied Scientific Research),
Anna van Buerenplein 1, 2595 DA, The Hague, The Netherlands
Email: maaike.deboer@tno.nl and jack.verhoosel@tno.nl

Abstract—**The manual creation of an ontology is a tedious task. In the field of ontology learning, Natural Language Processing (NLP) techniques are used to automatically create ontologies. In this paper, we present a methodology using data-driven techniques to create ontologies from unstructured documents in the agriculture domain. We use state-of-the-art NLP techniques based on Stanford OpenIE, Hearst patterns and co-occurrences to create ontologies. We add an NLP-method that uses dependency parsing and transformation rules based on linguistic patterns. In addition, we use keyword-driven techniques from the query expansion field, based on Word2vec, WordNet and ConceptNet, to create ontologies. We add a method that takes the union of the ontologies produced by the keyword-based methods. The semantic quality of the different ontologies is calculated using automatically extracted keywords. We define recall, precision and F1-score based on the concepts and relations in which the keywords are present. The results show that 1) the method based on co-occurrences has the best F1-score with more than 100 keywords; 2) the keyword-based methods have a higher F1-score than the NLP-based methods with less than 100 keywords in the evaluation and; 3) the combined keyword-based method always has a higher F1-score compared to each single method. In our future work, we will focus on improving the dependency parsing algorithm, improving combining different ontologies, and improving our quality evaluation methodology.**

Keywords–Knowledge engineering; Machine Learning; Agriculture.

I. Introduction

In the previous decade, data scientists often used either a knowledge-driven or a data-driven approach to create their models / classifiers. In the knowledge-driven approach, the (expert) knowledge is structured in a model, such as an ontology. Some advantages of this type of approach is that it is insightful, validated by experts, and it gives a feeling of control. Some disadvantages of the knowledge-driven approach are that it takes a lot of dedicated effort to construct the model, it is hard to provide the full model (only possible in closed-world domains) and that there might not be one truth [1]. If two experts create a knowledge model, they probably will come up with different ones, because each expert has his own subjective view of important concepts and relations in the domain. On the other hand, data-driven approaches do not need the dedicated effort from people to construct the model, because an algorithm is used that extracts a model much faster. Disadvantages of data-driven approaches is that the models are often not insightful, they might contain too much noise and might be less 'crisp'.

As knowledge-driven and data-driven approaches each have their advantages, a combination of both approaches is worthwhile to use. A field in which ontologies learn from available knowledge using data is named *ontology learning*. We present in this paper an ontology learning methodology that uses existing and new data-driven algorithms to create ontologies based on unstructured textual documents in the agriculture domain. This results in an initial ontology that serves as a good starting point for further improvement by experts in the domain. The goal of this methodology is to create an improved ontology that can be used for semantic interoperability between Internet Technology (IT) systems and human users. We use state-of-the-art techniques in ontology learning to create ontologies. Additionally, we use keyword-based techniques to create ontologies. These keywords are used to find relations in external knowledge bases and a word embedding model.

In order to evaluate the performance of our methodology, we measure the semantic quality of the resulting ontologies using a keyword-based method. We define recall, precision and F1-score based on automatically extracted keywords and their appearance in the ontologies. From a semantic point of view, the extracted ontology should therefore be evaluated on the number of important keywords it contains. From a usability point of view, it is important that the ontology is still comprehensible for the human user. We use a well-known keyword extraction algorithm to get the main keywords from the document set and limit the number of evaluation keywords in the ontology.

In the next section, we describe the related work on ontology learning and the evaluation of ontologies. In Section 3, we explain the methods used to create the different ontologies. Section 4 describes our evaluation methodology and presents our results and Section 5 contains a discussion and conclusion as well as a description of future work.

II. Related Work

A. *Ontology Learning*

Ontology learning is focused on learning ontologies based on data [2] [3]. One of the most known concepts in ontology learning is the ontology learning layer cake. Starting from the bottom of the cake, the order is terms, synonyms, concept formation, concept hierarchy, relations, relation hierarchy, axiom schemata and finally general axioms. Similar to the layed cake, Gillani et al. [4] describe the process of ontology learning by input, term extraction, concept extraction, relation extraction, concept categorization, evaluation, ontology mapping. Ontologies can be learned in three kind of manners: structured, semi-structured and unstructured data [2]. Besides the manner of learning, there are three types of tools available: ontology editing tools, ontology merging tools and ontology extraction tools [5]. In this paper, we want to automatically create ontologies from text, so we focus on unstructured data and ontology extraction tools.

Several tools are already available. Some tools only focus on the information extraction, up to the relation extraction part. This subfield is also named Open Information Extraction

(OpenIE). One of the first in this category is TextRunner [6]. TextRunner tags sentences with part-of-speech tags and noun phrase chunks, in a fast manner with one loop over all documents. The Resolver system does unsupervised clustering of the extractions to create sets of synonymous entities and relations. TextRunner was followed by WOE, ReVerb, KrakeN, EXEMPLAR, OLLIE, PredPatt, ClausIE, OpenIE4, CSD-IE, NESTIE, MinIE and Graphene [7]. Recently, deep learning methods, such as the encoder-decoder framework from Cui et al. [8] have been proposed.

Related to the OpenIE field, query expansion can also be used to find more concepts and relations [9]. This method is often used in the information retrieval field. The most common method is to use WordNet [10]. Boer et al. [1] [11] also use ConceptNet to find related concepts and their relations. Word2vec is also used in information retrieval [12], ontology enrichment [13] and ontology learning [14].

One of the oldest methods that use the full ontology learning layered cake seems to be Terminae [15]. Terminae is a method and platform for ontology engineering, and includes linguistic analysis with NLP tools to extract and select terms and relations, conceptual modeling / normalization (differentiation, alignment and restructuring) and formalization / model checking, with the syntactic and semantic validation.

OntoLT [16] is available as a plugin in Protégé and enables mapping rules. Linguistic annotation of text documents is done using Shallow and CHunk-based Unication Grammar tools (SCHUG) [17], which provide annotation of part-of-speech, morphological inflection and decomposition, phrase and dependency structure. The mapping rules can then be used to map the ontologies or the document into one ontology.

Text2Onto [18] uses GATE to extract entities. GATE [19] has a submodule named ANNIE that contains a tokeniser, sentence splitter, Part-of-Speech (POS) tagger, gazetteer, nite state transducer, orthomatcher and coreference resolver. Several metrics, such as Relative Term Frequency (RTF), Term Frequency Inverted Document Frequency (TF-IDF), Entropy and the C-value/NC-value are used to assess the relevance of a concept. The relations between concepts are found with WordNet, hearst patterns, and created patterns in JAPE. With the Probabilistic Ontology Model, the learned knowledge is stored at a meta-level in the form of instantiated modelling primitives. The model is, therefore, robust to different languages and changing information. According to Zouaq et al. [20], Text2Onto generates very shallow and light weight ontologies.

Concept-Relation-Concept Tuple based Ontology Learning (CRCTOL) [21] uses the Stanford POS tagger and the Berkeley parser to assign syntactic tags to the words. They use a Domain Relevance Measure (DRM), a combination of TF-IDF and likelihood ratio, to determine the relevance of a word or multi-word expression. LESK and VLESK are used for word sense disambiguation. Hearst patterns, relations in WordNet and created patterns with regular expressions are used to find relations with the relevant terms. According to Gillani et al. [4], CRCTOL only creates general concepts and ignores whole-part relations, the ontology is not the comprehensive and accurate representation of a given domain and it is time-consuming to run the tool, because it does full-text parsing.

CFinder [22] is created to automatically find key concepts in text. They use the Stanford POS tagger, a dictionary lookup for synonym finding, stopword removal, and combination of words to also have dependent phrases as concepts. The key concepts are then extracted using a rank-based algorithm that uses the tf (term frequency) and a domain specific df (document frequency) as weight. The paper stops at the key concept extraction and does not go further with determining relations.

OntoUPS [23] uses the Stanford dependency parser, and learns an Is-A hierarchy over clusters of logical expressions, and populates it by translating sentences to logical form. It uses Markov Logical Networks (MLNs) for that.

OntoCMaps [20] uses the Stanford POS tagger and dependency parser to extract concepts. It uses several generic patterns to extract relations.

Promine [4] uses tokenization, stop word filtering, lemmatization, and term frequency to create a set of key words. Wordnet, Wiktionary and a domain glossary (AGROVOC) are used for concept enrichment. The relevance, or term goodness, is calculated with the information gain, which combines the entropy and conditional probability. The concepts are filtered using the information gain, path length and depth of concepts.

More recently, Mittal et al. [24] combined knowledge graphs and vector spaces into a VKG structure. In that way, both a smart inference from the knowledge graphs and a fast look-up from the vector spaces are combined. This method, however, does not automatically create a new ontology from text documents.

Also deep learning is used in knowledge graphs. Schlichtkrull et al. [25] propose a Graph Convolutional Network to predict missing facts and missing entity attributes. This method can, thus, also not create an ontology from a set of documents, but is able to enrich an existing ontology.

B. Evaluating ontologies

Brank et al. [26] state that most approaches to evaluate ontologies can be place in one of the following categories:

- Golden Standard: compare to "golden standard"
- Application-based: use in application and evaluate results
- Data-driven: involve comparisons with a data source
- Assesment by humans: human evaluation based on a set of predefined criteria, standards, and / or requirements

Hlomani et al. [27] also uses these approaches in their survey, and state the advantages and disadvantages of each approach. We focus on the disadvantages of the approaches first. In the golden standard, the main disadvantage is the evaluation of the golden standard and the performance is highly dependent on the quality of the golden standard. In the application-based approach, the disadvantage is generalizability: what might be good in one application does not have to be good in another. The application-based approach is also only applicable for a small set of ontologies. The main disadvantage of the data-driven approach is that the domain knowledge is assumed to be constant, is not the case. Finally, the disadvantage of the human assessment is subjectivity.

In this paper, we focus on the data-driven evaluation. We do not have a golden standard, or an application, which leaves us with a data-driven or human assessment approach. In the data-driven approach the ontology is often compared against existing data about the domain. Many papers on this topic

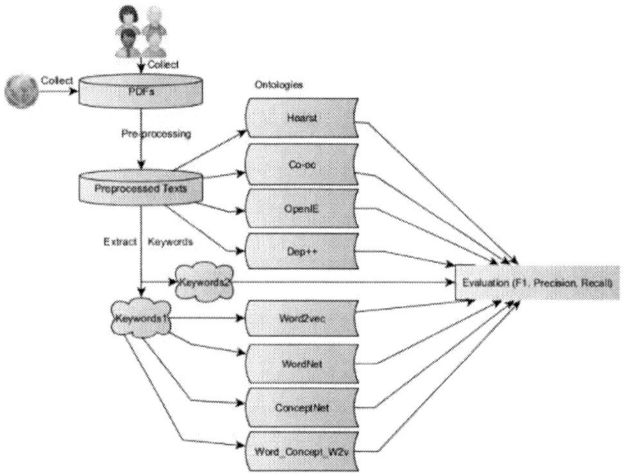

Figure 1. Overview of the methods to create the ontologies

focus on some kind of coverage of the domain knowledge within the ontology [28]–[31]. For example, Brewster et al. [31] compare extracted terms and relations from text with the concepts and relations in the ontology. They use a probabilistic model to determine the best ontology for a certain domain.

Besides the categories, ontologies can be evaluated on different levels. These levels are defined differently in different papers. Brank et al. [26] divides the levels in lexical, hierarchical, other semantic relations, context, syntactic, structure. They link the categories and the levels in a matrix, in which the human assessment is the only category which evaluates on all levels. The data-driven approach can only evaluate on the first three levels. The distinction of Burton et al. [32] is syntactic, semantic, pragmatic and social. Gangemi et al. [33] use the distinction between structural, functional and usability-profiling. Burton et al. [32] use lawfulness, richness, interpretability, consistency, clarity, comprehensiveness, accuracy, relevance, authority, and history. Lozano et al. [34] even use a three-level framework of 117 criteria. Hlomani et al. [27] make the distinction between ontology quality and ontology correctness views on ontology evaluation. For ontology quality, they focus on computational efficiency, adaptability and clarity. Ontology correctness uses accuracy, completeness, conciseness and consistency. Recently, Mcdaniel et al. [35] introduced the DOORS framework in which ontologies can be ranked by using syntactic, semantic, pragmatic and social quality metrics.

III. Method

In this paper, we create a taxonomy or concept hierarchy, and we do not include the top two layers of the layered cake (domain, range and axioms / generic rules). Figure 1 shows an overview of the methods used to create the ontologies. Our experts collected 135 articles on the Agriculture domain, including Agrifood, Agro-ecology, crop production and the food supply chain. From each article we first extracted the plain text from the PDF. On these plain texts we used sentence splitting, tokenizing, removing non-ascii and non-textual items as pre-processing. With these pre-processed texts we created the state-of-the-art ontologies Hearst, Co-oc and OpenIE (explained below). We also added a new method based on Dependencies and some rules.

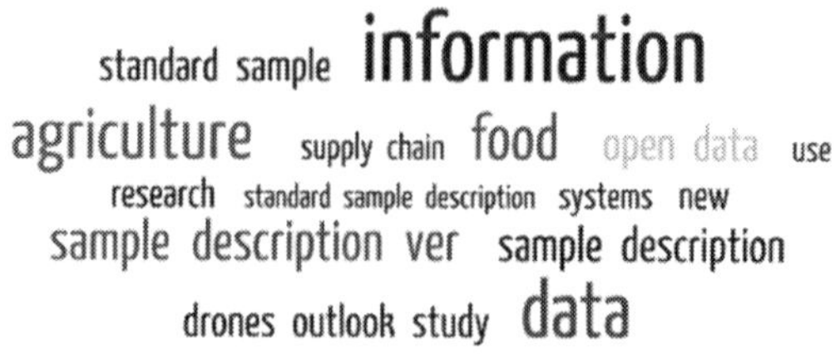

Figure 2. Terms Extracted with the method from Verberne et al. [36]

To create the keyword-driven ontologies, we needed to extract keywords. We used the Term Frequency (TF) and the term extraction method from Verberne et al. [36]. The result of this term extraction method is shown in Figure 2. The standard Wikipedia corpus from the paper is used as background set. We combined the keywords of the two sets and manually deleted all non-relevant terms, resulting in the following set of keywords: *Data, Food, Information, Drones, Agriculture, Crop, Technology, Agricultural, Production, Development, Farmers, Supply Chain*. These keywords were used to create the Word2vec, WordNet and ConceptNet ontologies.

a) Hearst: Hearst patterns [37] can be used to extract hyponym relations, represented in an ontology as a 'IsA' relation. An example is 'Vegetable' is a hyponym of 'Food'. In unstructured texts, hyponyms can be spotted using the lexical structures 'NP, such as NP', or 'NP, or other NP', where NP is a noun phrase. These patterns are used to create an ontology with 'IsA' relations.

b) Co-oc: Co-occurrences can extract all type of relations, because the number of times words co-occur with each other, for example in the same sentence, are counted [38]. We used a maximum distance of four words to calculate the co-occurrences. The ontology based on co-occurrences, thus, will have many classes and one vague relation, i.e. that the classes have co-occurred with each other in documents.

c) OpenIE: The Open Information Extraction tool (OpenIE) is created by the CoreNLP group of Stanford [39]. The tools from the Stanford CoreNLP group are one of the most used tools in the NLP field. The OpenIE tool provides the whole chain from plain text through syntactic analysis (sentence splitter, part-of-speech tagger, dependency parser) to triples (object - relation - subject). The extracted relations are often the verbs in the sentence, and this results in a lot of triples multiple word concepts and a lot of different relations.

d) Dep++: Similar to OntoCMaps [20], we use patterns to enhance the the Stanford Dependency Parser [40]. The algorithm consists of the following steps. Take each document in the corpus and generate sentences based on NLTK tokenization. Consider only sentences with more than 5 words which pass through the English check of the Python langdetect package. Parse each sentence through the Stanford DepParse annotator to generate Enhanced++Dependencies. Replace every word in the Enh++Dep by its lemma as produced by the Stanford POS tagger to consider only singular words. Then, generate a graph with a triple <governor,dependency,dependent> for each enhanced++dependency and apply the following transformation rules to the it.

- 1: Transform compound dependencies into 2-word concepts using rule: if $(X, compound, Y)$ then replace X with YX and remove Y

- 2: Enhance subject-object relations based on conjunction dependencies using rule: if $(X, nsubj, Y)$ and $(X, dobj, Z)$ and $(X, conj\_and, X')$ then add $(X', nsubj, Y)$ and $(X', dobj, Z)$

Finally, apply language patterns to derive triples from the dependency graph:

- pattern 1: if $(X, amod, Y)$ then add triple $(YX, subClassOf, X)$
- pattern 2: if $(X, compound, Y)$ and $(X \text{is} NN \text{or} NNS)$ then add triple $(YX, subClassOf, X)$
- pattern 3: if $(X, nsubj, Y)$ and $(X, dobj, Z)$ then add triple (Y, X, Z)

This algorithm yields an ontology that is similar to the OpenIE ontology, but should have less noise in it in terms of NLP-based constructs.

e) Word2vec: Word2vec is a group of models, which produce semantic embeddings. These models create neural word embeddings using a shallow neural network that is trained on a huge dataset, such as Wikipedia, Google News or Twitter. Each word vector is trained to maximize the log probability of neighboring words, resulting in a good performance in associations, such as *king - man + woman = queen*. We use the skip-gram model with negative sampling (SGNS) [41] to create a semantic embedding of our agriculture documents. With the keywords, we search for the top ten most similar words and add a 'RelatedTo' relation between the keyword and this most similar word. This process is repeated for all most similar words.

f) WordNet: WordNet is a hierarchical dictionary containing lexical relations between words, such as synonyms, hyponyms, hypernyms and antonyms [42]. It also provides all possible meanings of the word, which are called *synsets*, together with a short definition and usage examples. WordNet contains over 155,000 words and over 206,900 word-sense pairs. We use the keywords to search in WordNet. We select the first synset (the most common) and extract the 'Synonym' and 'Antonym' relations and use these to create our ontology.

g) ConceptNet: ConceptNet (5) is a knowledge representation project in which a semantic graph with general human knowledge is build [43]. This general human knowledge is collected using other knowledge bases, such as Wikipedia and WordNet, and experts and volunteers. Some of the relations in ConceptNet are *RelatedTo, IsA, partOf, HasA, UsedFor, CapableOf, AtLocation, Causes, HasSubEvent, CreatedBy, Synonym* and *DefinedAs*. The strength of the relation is determined by the amount and reliability of the sources asserting the fact. Currently, ConceptNet contains concepts from 77 language and more than 28 million links between concepts. We use the keywords to search (through the API) in ConceptNet and extract all direct relations to create the ontology.

h) Word_Concept_W2v: This method takes the union (all relations) from the keyword-based methods WordNet, ConceptNet and Word2vec.

IV. RESULTS

To evaluate the created ontologies we use a simple but effective keyword-based evaluation method based on the framework of Brewster et al. [31]. Our evaluation algorithm first generates a set of keywords *K* from the document set using the *KLDiv* term extraction algorithm [36]. Then, the assumption is that the semantic quality of an ontology is better if a keyword is present as concept in a relation in the ontology. If we define an ontology as being a set of relations *R* between concepts, then we can defined keyword-based recall, precision and F1-score as follows:

$$
\begin{aligned}
Prec &= \frac{\#r \in R \text{ with } k \in K}{\#r \in R} \\
Rec &= \frac{\#k \in K \text{ found in } R}{\#k \in K} \\
F1 &= 2 * \frac{(Rec * Prec)}{Rec + Prec}
\end{aligned}
\tag{1}
$$

where k is keyword in set of Keywords (K), r is relation in set of Relations (R). The set of selected items is thus the set of relations R (precision), and the set of relevant items is thus the set of keywords K (recall).

Figure 3 shows for each ontology the overall quality based on the F1 score for 15, 30, 50, 100, 150 and 200 keywords, Figure 4 and Figure 5 show the precison and recall. Table I shows the number of classes and some example of the relations with the word 'Agriculture'.

TABLE I. INSIGHTS IN THE DIFFERENT ONTOLOGIES.

OntologyName	#Classes	RelationAgriculture
Hearst	7523	sector, yield forecasting, irrigation
Co-oc	1049	food, woman, adopt, production
OpenIE	280,063	sustainability, they, vision, water use
Dep++	178,338	sustainable, industrial, we, climate-smart
Word2vec	234	farming, biofuel, horticulture, innovation
WordNet	113	agribusiness, factory farm, farming
ConceptNet	203	farm, farmer, class, agribusiness
Word_Concept_W2v	491	agribusiness, farming, farm, horticulture

The results show that the combined keyword-based methods (light-blue line) are always better than any of the three separate methods (WordNet, ConceptNet and Word2vec). The keyword-based methods have a higher F1 score with a lower number of keywords, whereas the NLP-based methods have a higher F1 score with a higher number of keywords. With 200 keywords, the best performing method is Co-oc, the method based on co-occurrences.

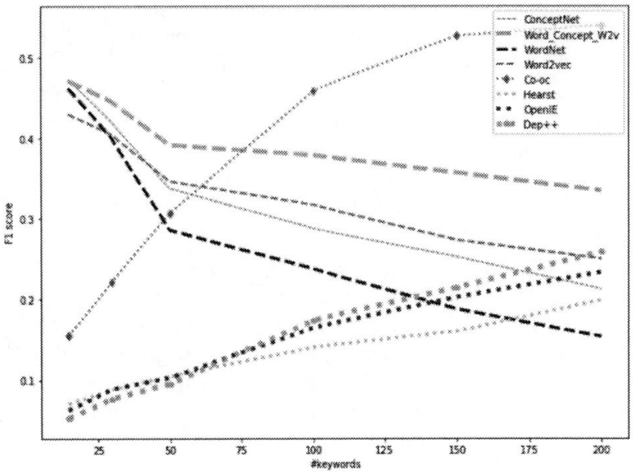

Figure 3. F1 score for the different methods

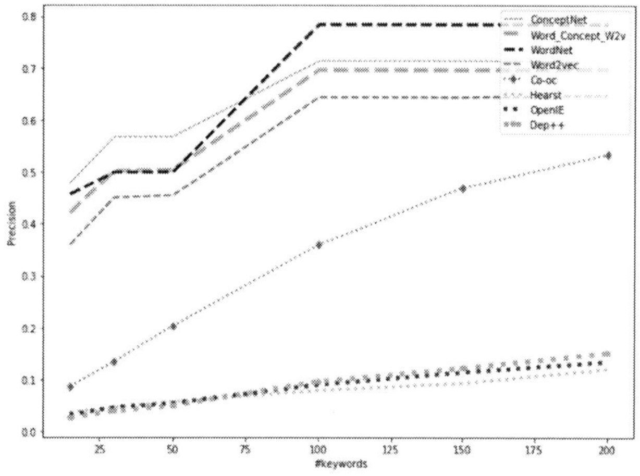

Figure 4. Precision score for the different methods

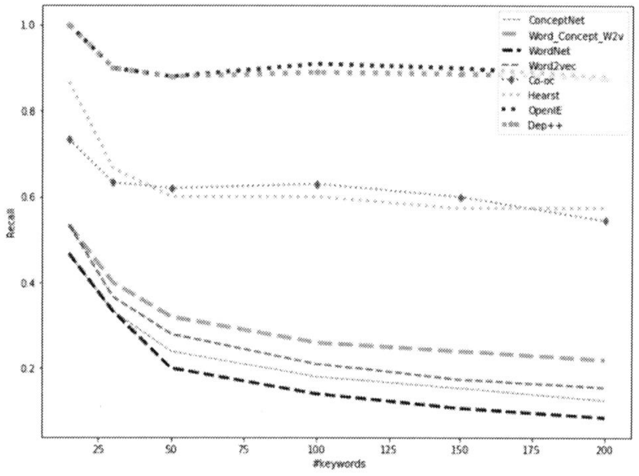

Figure 5. Recall score for the different methods

V. Discussion, Conclusion and Future Work

In this paper, we presented a methodology to use existing and new algorithms to create data-driven ontologies based on unstructured textual documents in the agriculture domain. In addition, we used a data-driven method based on keywords to evaluate the semantic quality of the ontologies. The goal of this methodology is to generate an initial ontology that serves as a good starting point for further improvement by experts in the domain. The resulting improved ontology can then be used for semantic interoperability between IT-systems and human users.

The results show that the keyword-based methods have the highest F1-score for less than 100 keywords. This can be validated by looking at the number of concepts. The keyword-based methods have less concepts than the NLP-based methods. If one keyword is found by the keyword-based methods, the precision will be already much higher than the precision of the NLP-based methods. When the number of evaluation-keywords increases the keyword-based methods perform less, because they contain less concepts. One critical note is that we based the keywords-based methods and the evaluation method on the same set of documents. Although we used a manual selection on the keywords and multiple keyword-based methods to find the set of keywords, we know that there might have been some overlap in the keywords used in creating the ontologies and the evaluation. This also clarifies why the performance on a few keywords is higher for the keyword-based methods. The NLP-based methods gain performance with more keywords in the evaluation. This is mainly due to the fact that the recall keeps about the same value, but the precision becomes higher, i.e. relatively more relevant relations are found and always divided by the same high number of relations.

The most outstanding method in that respect is the co-occurrences algorithm. Whereas the other NLP-methods have a precision of about 0.15, Co-occurrences can grow to 0.5. Although Hearst has a smaller number of concepts, the concepts and relations in Co-oc are better suited for the keyword-based evaluation method. When comparing the NLP-methods OpenIE and Dep++ alone, we can conclude that Dep++ performs slightly better then OpenIE. This is surprising as only a few NLP-patterns are used to generate the ontology based on the enhanced NLP-dependency relations.

Aside from the good gain in performance of Co-oc and the good performance of the keyword-based methods, we see that the combined keyword-based method is better than any of the single methods. This can mainly be explained by the higher recall: more related keywords are found when combining the methods, and therefore recall is higher. This is an indication that future work can be targeted to improvement of our ontology merging techniques on top of the union merge.

Based on these results, we consider the following possibilities for future work. First, a logical next step is improving the combination of multiple ontologies. Combining the keyword-based methods is logical as a union, but adding even more concepts and relations to the already big NLP-based ontologies might not be the best way forward. We could for example use some filtering, or seeding with keywords or an existig man-made ontology. Second, the Dep++ algorithm can be further improved by using other NLP-patterns known in the literature. This can improve the precision of this methodology, as the recall is already quite high. Third, another interesting next step is to improve on the quality evaluation method. We did some first experiments with the DOORS algorithm, but on some layers the results are not yet reliable. Using the keyword-based evaluation is objective and semantically sound, but because we use the same document set for creation and testing of the ontologies this might influence the performance.

Concluding, we made a first step towards automatically creating data-driven ontologies using a domain specific document set. We used and compared NLP-based and keyword-based techniques, and an exciting next step is to combine the best of both worlds to create even better ontologies.

Acknowledgment

This work has been executed as part of the Interreg Smart-Green project (https://northsearegion.eu/smartgreen/). The authors would like to thank Christopher Brewster for giving useful comments and providing a representative agriculture-related document set.

REFERENCES

[1] M. de Boer, K. Schutte, and W. Kraaij, "Knowledge based query expansion in complex multimedia event detection," Multimedia Tools and Applications, vol. 75, no. 15, 2016, pp. 9025–9043.

[2] P. Cimiano, A. Mädche, S. Staab, and J. Völker, "Ontology learning," in Handbook on ontologies. Springer, 2009, pp. 245–267.

[3] C. A. Brewster, "Mind the gap: Bridging from text to ontological knowledge," Ph.D. dissertation, University of Sheffield, 2008.

[4] S. Gillani and A. Kő, "Promine: a text mining solution for concept extraction and filtering," in Corporate Knowledge Discovery and Organizational Learning. Springer, 2016, pp. 59–82.

[5] J. Park, W. Cho, and S. Rho, "Evaluating ontology extraction tools using a comprehensive evaluation framework," Data & Knowledge Engineering, vol. 69, no. 10, 2010, pp. 1043–1061.

[6] A. Yates and et al., "Textrunner: open information extraction on the web," in Proceedings of Human Language Technologies: The Annual Conference of the North American Chapter of the Association for Computational Linguistics: Demonstrations. Association for Computational Linguistics, 2007, pp. 25–26.

[7] C. Niklaus, M. Cetto, A. Freitas, and S. Handschuh, "A survey on open information extraction," arXiv preprint arXiv:1806.05599, 2018.

[8] L. Cui, F. Wei, and M. Zhou, "Neural open information extraction," arXiv preprint arXiv:1805.04270, 2018.

[9] R. Alfred and et al., "Ontology-based query expansion for supporting information retrieval in agriculture," in The 8th International Conference on Knowledge Management in Organizations. Springer, 2014, pp. 299–311.

[10] M. Song, I.-Y. Song, X. Hu, and R. B. Allen, "Integration of association rules and ontologies for semantic query expansion," Data & Knowledge Engineering, vol. 63, no. 1, 2007, pp. 63–75.

[11] M. H. de Boer and et al., "Query interpretation–an application of semiotics in image retrieval," International Journal on Advances in Software, vol. 3 4, 2015, pp. 435–449.

[12] M. H. De Boer, Y.-J. Lu, H. Zhang, K. Schutte, C.-W. Ngo, and W. Kraaij, "Semantic reasoning in zero example video event retrieval," ACM Transactions on Multimedia Computing, Communications, and Applications (TOMM), vol. 13, no. 4, 2017, p. 60.

[13] İ. Pembeci, "Using word embeddings for ontology enrichment," International Journal of Intelligent Systems and Applications in Engineering, vol. 4, no. 3, 2016, pp. 49–56.

[14] G. Wohlgenannt and F. Minic, "Using word2vec to build a simple ontology learning system," in International Semantic Web Conference (Posters & Demos), 2016.

[15] B. Biebow, S. Szulman, and A. J. Clément, "Terminae: A linguistics-based tool for the building of a domain ontology," in Int. Conf. on Knowledge Engineering and Knowledge Management. Springer, 1999, pp. 49–66.

[16] P. Buitelaar, D. Olejnik, and M. Sintek, "A protégé plug-in for ontology extraction from text based on linguistic analysis," in European Semantic Web Symposium. Springer, 2004, pp. 31–44.

[17] T. Declerck, "A set of tools for integrating linguistic and non-linguistic information," in Proceedings of SAAKM (ECAI Workshop), 2002.

[18] P. Cimiano and J. Völker, "text2onto," in Int. Conf. on Appl. of Nat. Lang. to Inf. Sys. Springer, 2005, pp. 227–238.

[19] H. Cunningham, D. Maynard, K. Bontcheva, and V. Tablan, "Gate: an architecture for development of robust hlt applications," in Proceedings of the 40th annual meeting on association for computational linguistics. Association for Computational Linguistics, 2002, pp. 168–175.

[20] A. Zouaq, "An overview of shallow and deep natural language processing for ontology learning," in Ontology learning and knowledge discovery using the web: Challenges and recent advances. IGI Global, 2011, pp. 16–37.

[21] X. Jiang and A.-H. Tan, "Crctol: A semantic-based domain ontology learning system," Journal of the American Society for Information Science and Technology, vol. 61, no. 1, 2010, pp. 150–168.

[22] Y.-B. Kang, P. D. Haghighi, and F. Burstein, "Cfinder: An intelligent key concept finder from text for ontology development," Expert Systems with Applications, vol. 41, no. 9, 2014, pp. 4494–4504.

[23] H. Poon and P. Domingos, "Unsupervised ontology induction from text," in Proceedings of the 48th annual meeting of the Association for Computational Linguistics. Association for Computational Linguistics, 2010, pp. 296–305.

[24] S. Mittal, A. Joshi, T. Finin et al., "Thinking, fast and slow: Combining vector spaces and knowledge graphs," arXiv, no. arXiv: 1708.03310, 2017.

[25] M. Schlichtkrull, T. N. Kipf, P. Bloem, R. van den Berg, I. Titov, and M. Welling, "Modeling relational data with graph convolutional networks," in European Semantic Web Conference. Springer, 2018, pp. 593–607.

[26] J. Brank, M. Grobelnik, and D. Mladenić, "A survey of ontology evaluation techniques," 2005.

[27] H. Hlomani and D. Stacey, "Approaches, methods, metrics, measures, and subjectivity in ontology evaluation: A survey," Semantic Web Journal, vol. 1, no. 5, 2014, pp. 1–11.

[28] P. Spyns, "Evalexon: Assessing triples m ined from texts," STAR, vol. 9, 2005, p. 09.

[29] H. Hlomani and D. A. Stacey, "Contributing evidence to data-driven ontology evaluation workflow ontologies perspective," in 5th International Conference on Knowledge Engineering and Ontology Development, KEOD 2013, 2013, pp. 207–213.

[30] L. Ouyang, B. Zou, M. Qu, and C. Zhang, "A method of ontology evaluation based on coverage, cohesion and coupling," in Fuzzy Systems and Knowledge Discovery (FSKD), 2011 Eighth International Conference on, vol. 4. IEEE, 2011, pp. 2451–2455.

[31] C. Brewster, H. Alani, S. Dasmahapatra, and Y. Wilks, "Data driven ontology evaluation," 2004.

[32] A. Burton-Jones, V. C. Storey, V. Sugumaran, and P. Ahluwalia, "A semiotic metrics suite for assessing the quality of ontologies," Data & Knowledge Engineering, vol. 55, no. 1, 2005, pp. 84–102.

[33] A. Gangemi and V. Presutti, "Ontology design patterns," in Handbook on ontologies. Springer, 2009, pp. 221–243.

[34] A. Lozano-Tello and A. Gómez-Pérez, "Ontometric: A method to choose the appropriate ontology," Journal of Database Management (JDM), vol. 15, no. 2, 2004, pp. 1–18.

[35] M. McDaniel, V. C. Storey, and V. Sugumaran, "Assessing the quality of domain ontologies: Metrics and an automated ranking system," Data & Knowledge Engineering, vol. 115, 2018, pp. 32–47.

[36] S. Verberne, M. Sappelli, D. Hiemstra, and W. Kraaij, "Evaluation and analysis of term scoring methods for term extraction," Information Retrieval Journal, vol. 19, no. 5, 2016, pp. 510–545.

[37] M. A. Hearst, "Automatic acquisition of hyponyms from large text corpora," in Proceedings of the 14th conference on Computational linguistics-Volume 2. Association for Computational Linguistics, 1992, pp. 539–545.

[38] Y. Matsuo and M. Ishizuka, "Keyword extraction from a single document using word co-occurrence statistical information," International Journal on Artificial Intelligence Tools, vol. 13, no. 01, 2004, pp. 157–169.

[39] G. Angeli, M. J. J. Premkumar, and C. D. Manning, "Leveraging linguistic structure for open domain information extraction," in Proc. of 53 ACL and 7th Int. Joint Conf. on NLP (Vol 1: Long Papers), vol. 1, 2015, pp. 344–354.

[40] M.-C. De Marneffe, B. MacCartney, and C. D. Manning, "Generating typed dependency parses from phrase structure parses," 2006.

[41] T. Mikolov, I. Sutskever, K. Chen, G. S. Corrado, and J. Dean, "Distributed representations of words and phrases and their compositionality," in Adv. in neural information processing systems, 2013, pp. 3111–3119.

[42] G. A. Miller, "Wordnet: a lexical database for english," Communications of the ACM, vol. 38, no. 11, 1995, pp. 39–41.

[43] R. Speer and C. Havasi, "Representing general relational knowledge in conceptnet 5." in LREC, 2012, pp. 3679–3686.